10
Strategies
for
Doubling
Student
Performance

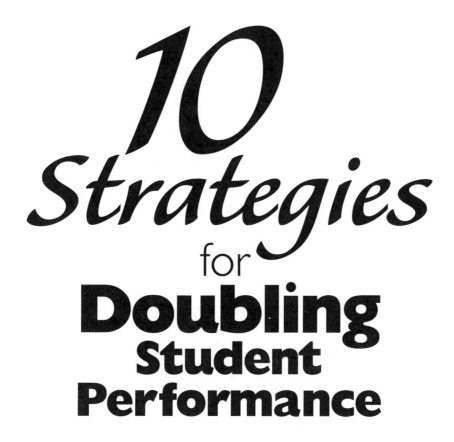

10
Strategies
for
Doubling
Student
Performance

Allan R. Odden

CORWIN
A SAGE Company

For information:

Corwin
A SAGE Company
2455 Teller Road
Thousand Oaks, California 91320
(800) 233-9936
Fax: (800) 417-2466
www.corwinpress.com

SAGE India Pvt. Ltd.
B 1/I 1 Mohan Cooperative
   Industrial Area
Mathura Road, New Delhi 110 044
India

SAGE Ltd.
1 Oliver's Yard
55 City Road
London EC1Y 1SP
United Kingdom

SAGE Asia-Pacific Pte. Ltd.
33 Pekin Street #02-01
Far East Square
Singapore 048763

Printed in the United States of America.

Library of Congress Cataloging-in-Publication Data

Odden, Allan.
10 strategies for doubling student performance / Allan R. Odden.
      p. cm.
Includes bibliographical references and index.
ISBN 978-1-4129-7147-8 (cloth)
ISBN 978-1-4129-7148-5 (pbk.)
    1. Academic achievement—United States. 2. School improvement programs—United States. 3. School-based management—United States—Case studies. 4. Education—Economic aspects—United States. 5. Educational change—United States—Case studies.
I. Title. II. Title: Ten strategies for doubling student performance.

LB1062.6.O32 2009
371.2'07—dc22   2009019958

This book is printed on acid-free paper.

09   10   11   12   13   10   9   8   7   6   5   4   3   2   1

Acquisitions Editor:	Debra Stollenwerk
Associate Editor:	Julie McNall
Production Editor:	Cassandra Margaret Seibel
Copy Editor:	Nancy Conger
Typesetter:	C&M Digitals (P) Ltd.
Proofreader:	Charlotte J. Waisner
Indexer:	Jean Casalegno
Cover Designer:	Karine Hovsepian

Contents

Preface

The goal of this book is to show how schools and districts can produce large improvements in student academic achievement. By "large improvements" I mean in many cases a literal doubling of student performance as measured by state tests. Generically, the book uses "doubling" performance to connote large, quantum, absolute gains in student achievement. For example, doubling performance could mean increasing the percentage of students who score at or above the proficiency level from below average levels to much higher levels, such as from 30 to 60% or 35 to 70%. Though increasing such a percentage from 5 to 10%, or from 10 to 20%, represents a doubling of performance, all of the cases and studies in the book reference sites that started at a much higher level and then doubled performance. The phrase "doubling performance" also would include strategies for doubling the percentage achieving at or above the advanced levels, which should be the goal in many states where the state proficiency level is closer in rigor to the basic level of performance of the National Assessment of Education Progress (NAEP). For districts starting at higher levels of student performance, the definition of doubling would include a district or school increasing the percentage scoring at or above proficiency from 65 to 95%; even though not literally a doubling, such an increase represents large, absolute gains. Though the phrase "doubling performance" seems like an overpromise to many academics and even some practitioners, in the lay and policy communities it clearly communicates a message of large, significant, and measurable improvement, which is what parents, policymakers, and the public want.

Drawing from research I have conducted—research conducted by staff in the University of Wisconsin–Madison offices of the Consortium for Policy Research in Education (CPRE), research conducted by staff (including the author) involved with the consulting firm of Lawrence O. Picus and Associates as part of school finance adequacy studies, as well as research by others that has been published largely elsewhere (e.g., Blankstein, 2004; Chenoweth, 2007; Fielding, Kerr, & Rosier, 2004; Fullan, Hill, & Crévola, 2006; Herman et al., 2008; Hightower, Knapp, Marsh, & McLaughlin,

2002; Odden & Archibald, 2009; Odden et al., 2007; Supovitz, 2006; Waters & Vargo, 2008; Wise, 2008)—this book identifies and discusses the details of 10 major strategies districts and schools use to make dramatic improvements in student academic achievement. Surprisingly, all of this research has found that, though the specifics differ, the general strategies schools and districts have used to produce large, measurable gains in student performance are quite similar, regardless of school size, metropolitan or geographic location or sociodemographic characteristics.

To implement any powerful education improvement strategy with the goal of doubling student performance, a system needs not only the ten strategies discussed in this book but also both a budget plan and a human capital plan as part of its overall implementation plan. A previous book I recently coauthored with Sarah Archibald reviews the key elements of the budget plan that are needed (Odden & Archibald, 2009).

This book ends with a discussion of the human capital plan that is a foundation for any school and district implementing new educational improvement programs designed to double performance. It argues that the powerful strategies described in the book require talent to implement them and discusses how that talent can be found, particularly by urban schools and districts with large numbers of low-income and minority students, many of which have been lacking in teacher and principal talent.

AUDIENCE

The audience for this book is teachers, teacher leaders, principals, central office curriculum and professional development staff, and superintendents, as well as college and university classes that address school improvement issues, professional development, and the principalship. The book also would be useful for professional learning communities in districts and schools working to determine how to improve student performance; professional learning communities would be the engines that drive the 10-coach passenger train described in this book. School board members, legislators, and legislative staff, as well as education policy analysts also should be interested in this book, as it has many local and state policy implications and, when combined with the budget elements of the Odden and Archibald (2009) book, can be used to decide how to use scarce resources, particularly at the school level.

THE CONTEXT OF EDUCATION REFORM TODAY

For the past two decades, the United States has been engaged in ambitious and far-reaching education reforms. The rationales cited for reform include reasons of international economic competitiveness and enhanced economic and family opportunities for individuals, as well as the moral imperative of an equal and adequate public education as a stepping-stone to postsecondary educational opportunities, high-wage jobs, and civic progress and comity. The prime education goal in the twenty-first century is to educate the vast majority of all children to rigorous student performance levels. This goal includes high levels of attainment for low-income and minority children, as well as for all girls and boys. The aspiration is to have children learn to "world class" performance standards—to be able to know, think, problem solve, and communicate at high proficiency levels in all major subjects, including mathematics, science, reading/English/language arts/writing, history, and geography.

The education system will need to implement multiple and complex changes in order for the country to attain these lofty goals. Change will be required in school and classroom organization, curriculum programs, instructional practices, professional development, use of computer and information technologies, the allocation of fiscal resources, and the way education systems recruit, develop, and manage their most important talent—teachers and principals.

Though there is growing knowledge about what can be done by schools and districts to dramatically improve student performance, many are not aware of such strategies. By drawing on research that I and others around the country have conducted on places that have produced large and measurable gains in student academic learning, generally as measured by scores on state tests, this book outlines the key strategies that all schools and districts can deploy to attain those same goals.

This book complements the Corwin book published in 2009 by Odden and Archibald entitled *Doubling Student Performance . . . and Finding the Resources to Do It*, by going into more depth on the processes and strategies that have been used. This book does not address the resource issues but refers to the Odden and Archibald (2009) book for those interested in the resource dimensions of the strategies. How to turn those resource needs into an adequately funded state school finance system is described in the textbook I coauthor with Lawrence O. Picus (Odden & Picus, 2008).

The arguments and processes discussed in this book reinforce those who argue that schools and districts have significant control over issues that can lead to dramatic improvements in student learning. As such, it is a counterpoint to a movement for "bigger and bolder" education reforms that focus on issues outside of education such as reducing poverty, improving health care, making neighborhoods safer, and starting young children in preschool. The book shows that even when these other issues remain problems in the local school community, schools can still execute multiple aligned strategies that have been shown to have large positive impacts on student learning. This book certainly does not oppose those other, complementary, initiatives to improve conditions of children and families now in poverty, but it stresses the many, many actions schools and districts can implement *now* to improve student learning. I would argue that the steps outlined in this book compose the big and bold education reforms that parents and the public should insist be put into place in all schools *now* and that over time can be complemented by other programs that enhance family income, children's health, and community living conditions so they reinforce what occurs in schools.

Of course, the above line of argument assumes that there is knowledge about what works in education and that district and school leaders want to know what those strategies and programs are. Does such knowledge exist? As suggested in the previous paragraph, there is a strident debate occurring within the ranks of those who study and work in schools. One group argues that schools cannot do it all, and poverty, health care, and other issues need to be addressed before schools can make a big difference. Another group argues that schools need more money, smaller classes, and more involved parents.

Though I support the noneducation initiatives proposed by the first group and know that in some instances more money is needed, I side with those who have concluded that many of the challenges that schools face in improving student performance are created by the systems themselves:

- Our system often gives the districts and schools with the most difficult educational challenges inadequate funding.
- The education system too often does not recruit top teacher and leadership talent and simply takes what is left in August after most individuals with talent have accepted jobs in other districts.
- The education system too often puts too many inexperienced and undertrained teachers into the most challenging classrooms in high-poverty schools and communities.
- Too many teachers do not teach all elements of a rigorous curriculum and reduce expectations for student performance.
- Too many districts waste teacher and student time "prepping" students to take state tests rather than simply teaching them what they need to learn in authentic ways.
- Professional development is too often a mile wide and an inch deep with little or no impact on instructional practice and student learning.
- Most problematic, too often schools shortchange students from poverty backgrounds by not setting high goals and thereby not even trying to double their performance.

In short, there are many education system actions that could be changed and if changed in the directions outlined in this book would alter student performance and produce significant gains for the education system.

As this book shows, and for those who have read my writings over the years, it is clear that I have concluded that we know a substantial amount about what works in education, from how kids learn complex material to strategies districts and schools can implement to boost—literally double in some case—performance. I take this perspective, believing that there is considerable research on how all children can learn complex materials, with this knowledge being nicely summarized in a series of books from the National Research Council (Bransford, Brown, & Cocking, 1999; Donovan & Bransford, 2005a, 2005b, 2005c). Further, there is extensive research on individual programs that work such as, for example, comprehensive preschool for children aged three and four, small classes in the early elementary grades, individual and small-group tutoring, curriculum-based professional development, and academic-focused summer school (for a review, see Odden & Picus, 2008, chap. 4).

Moreover, there is increasing research, from multiple sources, on schools and districts that have "put it all together" and dramatically improved student performance, with many districts and schools actually doubling student achievement over a four- to six-year time period (e.g., Blankstein, 2004: Chenoweth, 2007; Fielding et al., 2004; Fullan et al., 2006; Herman et al., 2008; Hightower et al., 2002; Odden & Archibald, 2009; Odden et al., 2007; Supovitz, 2006; Wise, 2008). The winners of the Broad Prize in urban education show that large urban districts can boost student performance by large amounts; the winners, including Boston; Brownsville, Texas; Garden Grove and Long Beach, California; and New York City, are testimony to what can actually happen on the upside in urban education. These are not a few isolated instances of high performance; they represent scores and scores of schools and districts all over the country producing large gains in student achievement. As a result, they represent dozens of "existence proofs" that schools can make a large difference *now*, even though more funding is probably needed in many cases and other social, economic, and health policies could augment these education system advances.

To be sure, the education system probably does not have sufficient knowledge to educate *all* students to proficiency at world-class standards. But I argue and show in this book that there is sufficient knowledge to start now and make giant strides toward that goal. The primary evidence derives from districts and schools that have restructured their school program and in many cases literally doubled student performance in the process, paying for many of the changes through resource reallocation and deploying any new resources to their powerful new education improvement strategies. The book draws from the cases discussed in the Odden and Archibald (2009) book and enhanced with other case material from more recent studies, conducted mainly by the UW–Madison CPRE group, of Boston, Long Beach, Montgomery County Public Schools, and the Aldine school system outside of Houston—all urban districts with large numbers of students from poverty and minority backgrounds.

ORGANIZATION OF THE BOOK

The book is divided into 11 chapters. The first nine chapters discuss the details of each of the 10 elements used to double student performance. Chapter 10 discusses the talent and human capital management issues that compose the "people" side of implementing the 10 steps.[1] And Chapter 11 puts it all together and describes in summary what the dramatically improving school does.

Chapter 1 identifies the first strategy as understanding the performance problem and the challenges to improve performance that face most schools in America, particularly schools with large numbers of low-income and minority children. It documents this first step as critical and as the key first step of any large-scale, organizational change process, which certainly is the case for a system seeking to double student performance. The chapter not only argues that this step is key but also identifies how various schools and districts engaged in this step by implementing multiple initiatives aimed at helping all key staff understand the performance status/problems of the school or district and fully understand the distance between current and desired performance. This chapter also discusses the multiple factors that stimulated several schools and districts to engage in the process of doubling student performance and reallocating resources, as many people often ask what it takes to get more schools and districts to adopt the agenda of making dramatic improvements in student performance. Finally, the chapter notes that in most cases, the emphasis in this strategy is on analyzing student performance data and not student demographics, because schools can impact student performance but cannot change demographics.

Chapter 2 discusses the second strategy, which is setting very high and ambitious goals regardless of the current performance level or student demographics. One key aspect of schools and districts that make a big difference in student performance is that they set goals to make large differences. This chapter makes this point and identifies the various ways schools and districts have expressed these goals. It notes that although many of the schools and districts enroll large concentrations of low-income and minority students, these schools clearly have not been influenced negatively by those demographics. They believe all kids—including the kids in their classrooms—can learn to high standards; they set very ambitious goals for the future performance of their children, goals that are even more ambitious than "stretch goals"; and they attain those lofty goals in most instances.

Chapter 3 addresses the core educational issues that are the prime issues educators in schools can change: the curriculum and instructional program. Schools that produce high levels of student performance focus on what they can impact—everything that happens in schools: recruitment and selection of teachers; the assignment of teachers; the organization of curriculum and instruction; academic expectations; the specific curriculum, textbook, and instructional materials used; and instructional practice. They do not focus on poverty, the lack of health care for many urban children, problems with parent involvement, full funding of No Child Left Behind (NCLB), the problems with the state testing system or the accountability glitches of NCLB, and others. They address the pieces of the education system over which they have control. And that allows them to act. This chapter identifies multiple curriculum programs that have been adopted, some new Web-based curriculum and instructional tools that have been used, as well as the visions of effective instructional practice these districts create.[2]

Chapters 4 discusses the fact that all schools and districts making large improvements in student performance go beyond analyzing just state tests and administer and use a variety of additional measures of student performance—benchmark and formative assessments. This chapter describes several of these instruments, including those such as the Measures of Academic Progress (MAP) from the Northwest Evaluation Association (NWEA) and the Wireless Generation that have made their formative assessment systems available on hand-held computer devices with the results linked to Web-based professional development systems. The chapter makes the point that while no set of state tests are perfect, the places producing gains in student learning go far beyond state tests, incorporate more data on student performance, and use it in implementing a cycle of continuous instructional improvement that continuously toggles between data on student performance—formative, benchmark, or summative—and curriculum and instructional strategies, and their impacts on student achievement.

Chapter 5 identifies the intensive and ongoing professional development programs and strategies implemented by these schools and districts. This was a uniform finding from all schools and districts that we and others have studied, and it makes good sense. Often, the initial analysis of state testing data requires some professional development, as not all teachers and principals are skilled in analyzing the meaning of state test data. Further, the adoption of new curriculum programs requires additional professional development to help all teachers acquire the expertise to teach the new curricular materials well; moreover, most of the professional development linked to the new textbooks and other curriculum materials was provided by district staff or other consultants, not by the textbook companies. In addition, extensive and ongoing professional development is needed as the schools and districts work to develop the system's new approach to good instruction; such professional development around new instructional practices continues for several years and has not stopped in any of the places we studied that doubled performance. Finally, considerable professional development is needed on how to take the information from the formative assessments and design instructional programs that meet the needs of the students in each classroom.

Chapter 6 describes how the schools and districts used time more effectively and efficiently. Since time is virtually a "fixed" school resource, the chapter discusses the multiple ways that schools and districts took this fixed resource—about six hours of daily instruction over about 180 days of the school year—and used it to help them attain the goal of having all kids, but particularly the children in the middle and bottom, achieve at much higher levels. This chapter also describes the time and staffing needs of good professional development programs and identifies several ways schools and districts found and used time during the day for "job-embedded, ongoing" professional development.

Chapter 7 illustrates how all the districts and schools provided multiple extra help strategies for students struggling to achieve to proficiency or even higher performance standards. Some of these strategies are also ways of using time more effectively, and thus some of these strategies are discussed in Chapter 6 as well. The extra supports reflect a strong American value of giving multiple opportunities for its citizens to accomplish certain goals, in this case learning to a rigorous performance standard. But these extra help strategies also reflect a long-held theory of learning—namely, that given sufficient time, most students can learn to high standards. The combined strategies represent the concrete ways these places provided extended-learning time but held performance standards constant. Extra help and time were provided during the regular school day and year, outside the regular school day, and outside the regular school year, and the chapter describes these multiple, extra-help strategies.

Chapter 8 describes how these schools and districts created professional and collaborative school cultures inside the school—what some refer to as "professional learning communities" (PLCs)—as they implemented all their strategies. The chapter argues that these school/district cultures were largely a product of the activities discussed in the previous chapters, not something created by the schools and districts before engaging in the processes to double student performance. However, because the schools and districts engaged in the doubling performance processes in collaborative approaches from Step 1 onward, the leaders understood that the way to attain their ambitious goals was to proceed in a professional and not bureaucratic manner, with the goal over time of developing a collaborative and professional school culture—that is, a PLC. The chapter also identifies what education system leaders can do to create the conditions that support the effective operation of professional cultures and PLCs. This chapter also describes how the schools and districts created and used widespread instructional leadership by teachers, principals, and central office staff, a strategy often called "distributed leadership" in the educational research literature. This chapter identifies the various types of leadership roles played by different actors and spends some time arguing that since principals often cannot engage in all the instructional leadership roles that are needed many successful principals move teachers into such instructional positions, such as instructional facilitators or professional development coaches.

Chapter 9 describes why I call the schools and districts that doubled student performance "professional organizations." The organizations that doubled performance were professional organizations because they actively sought, from sources outside of the school, research evidence about how to improve schools, best practices from other schools and districts, and the top experts on how to provide the best reading, mathematics, science, and professional development programs. No school or district studied by others or us produced such large improvements in student performance relying on just their own knowledge. This chapter describes various ways schools and districts reached out to the professional education community to get the best and most current knowledge and practice and brought that into their schools to strengthen their overall improvement strategies.

Chapter 10 discusses the talent and human capital management issues underneath these school and district strategies to improve performance, focusing mainly on the talent challenges for large, urban districts. To improve student performance, schools and districts need a powerful education improvement strategy, the main features of which are discussed in the first nine chapters, but they also need the talent to execute the strategy. Sufficient teacher and principal talent often is not present; so this chapter discusses, mainly for urban schools and districts with talent shortages, what strategies can be launched to get the needed talent. It notes that this human capital side of improving student learning is very important but often not discussed; it also shows how schools and districts in the most impoverished communities can acquire talented teachers and principals.[3]

Chapter 11 functions as a short summary of all preceding chapters and describes in brief all the moving parts of a school that are continuously improving and that can, over the medium term, double student performance.

Finally, the table on the following pages functions as a quick reference guide to all the school and district examples throughout the text. This at-a-glance table lists all the schools and districts, identifies the size of each district, and then categorizes each as rural, urban, suburban, and secondary or elementary (or both).

NOTES

1. Chapter 10 discusses the issue of talent acquisition primarily for urban districts, as that is what my colleagues and I researched over the past two years. Hopefully, in the future, we or others will research this issue for rural districts as well, as they also have talent shortages.

2. The text identifies several specific curriculum programs and textbooks that have been adopted; this should not be necessarily taken as an endorsement of these programs by the author, who is simply reporting what the districts and schools did. Further, many times the schools and districts stated that they adopted "research-based" programs, and the text simply reports these statements without analyzing the pluses and minuses of any research that might have been referenced.

3. Again, this chapter focuses exclusively on urban districts because those were the districts studied on this issue.

(Continued)

Acknowledgments

Corwin gratefully acknowledges the contributions of the following reviewers:

Judy Brunner
Author, Consultant
Instructional Solutions Group
Springfield, Missouri

Addie Gaines
Elementary Principal
Kirbyville Elementary, Kirbyville R-6 School District
Kirbyville, Missouri

Douglas Gordon Hesbol
Superintendent
Laraway CCSD 70C
Joliet, Illinois

Glen Ishiwata
Superintendent
Moreland School District
San Jose, California

Lynn Lisy-Macan
Superintendent
Cobleskill-Richmondville Central School
Cobleskill, New York

About the Author

 **Allan R. Odden** is codirector of Strategic Management of Human Capital (SMHC) in public education, a project of the Consortium for Policy Research in Education (CPRE). The mission of SMHC is to improve student achievement and reduce achievement gaps by getting more powerful instructional practices into all classrooms through reform and restructuring of state and district human resource management systems, focusing initially on the country's largest 100 districts, most of which are urban.

He also is professor of educational leadership and policy analysis at the University of Wisconsin–Madison. He also is codirector of the Consortium for Policy Research in Education (CPRE). CPRE is a consortium of the University of Wisconsin–Madison, Pennsylvania, Harvard, Michigan, Northwestern, Teachers College–Columbia, and Stanford Universities. He formerly was professor of education policy and administration at the University of Southern California (1984–1993) and director of Policy Analysis for California Education (PACE), an education policy consortium of USC, Stanford, and the University of California, Berkeley.

He is an international expert on the management of human capital in education, teacher compensation, education finance, school-based financing, resource allocation and use, educational policy, school-based management, and educational policy implementation. He worked with the Education Commission of the States for a decade, serving as assistant executive director, director of policy analysis and research, and director of its educational finance center. He was president of the American Educational Finance Association in 1979–1980 and received AEFA's distinguished Service Award in 1998. He served as research director for special state educational finance projects in Connecticut (1974–1975), Missouri (1975–1977), South Dakota (1975–1977), New York (1979–1981), Texas (1988), New Jersey (1991), Missouri (1992–1993), the Joint Interim Task Force on School Finance Adequacy in Arkansas (2003, 2005), the Wyoming Select Committee on Finance (2005), Washington Learns (2006), and Wisconsin (2005–2007). He was appointed Special Court Master to the Remand Judge in the New Jersey *Abbott v. Burke* school finance court case for 1997 and 1998. He has worked on teacher compensation changes in dozens of states and districts. He currently is directing research projects on school finance adequacy, school finance redesign, resource reallocation in schools, the costs of instructional improvement, teacher compensation, and the strategic management of human capital in public education. Odden has written widely, publishing over 200 journal articles, book chapters, and research reports and 32 books and monographs. He has consulted for governors, state legislators, chief state school officers, national and local unions, the National Alliance for Business, the Business Roundtable, New American Schools, the U.S. Congress, the U.S. Secretary of Education, many local school districts, the state departments of education in Victoria and Queensland, Australia, and the Department for Education and Employment in England.

His most recent books include *Doubling Student Performance . . . and Finding the Resources to Do It* (Corwin, 2009) with Sarah Archibald; *School Finance: A Policy Perspective* (McGraw-Hill, 2008), with Lawrence O. Picus and *How to Create World Class Teacher Compensation* (Freeload Press, 2007) with Marc Wallace. Other books include *Paying Teachers for What They Know and Do: New and Smarter Compensation Strategies to Improve Schools* (Corwin, 1997, 2002) with Carolyn Kelley; *Reallocating Resources: How to Boost Student Achievement Without Spending More* (Corwin, 2001) with Sarah Archibald; *School Finance: A Policy Perspective* (McGraw-Hill, 1992, 2000, 2004) coauthored with Lawrence Picus; *School-Based Finance* (Corwin, 1999) edited with Margaret Goertz; *Financing Schools for High Performance: Strategies for Improving the Use of Educational Resources* (Jossey-Bass, 1998) with Carolyn Busch; *Educational Leadership for America's Schools* (McGraw-Hill, 1995); *Rethinking School Finance: An Agenda for the 1990s* (Jossey-Bass, 1992); *Education Policy Implementation* (State University of New York Press, 1991); and *School Finance and School Improvement: Linkages for the 1980s* (Ballinger, 1983).

He was a mathematics teacher and curriculum developer in New York City's East Harlem for five years. He received his PhD and MA degrees from Columbia University, a master of divinity degree from the Union Theological Seminary, and his BS in aerospace engineering from Brown University. He is married and has two children and one grandchild.

Understanding the Performance Challenge

Schools and districts do not engage in the multiple, organizationally complex and personally challenging actions to "double student performance" unless there is a perceived need to make such dramatic change. Teachers, principals, and school leaders must fully understand and want to address the performance challenge. As Kotter (1996) put it in his motivational book on leading large-scale change in organizations, people must feel a "sense of urgency" to engage in such processes. Doubling performance requires a sense of urgency to do so. And accomplishing that goal takes several years of focus on that task, exceptionally hard work, and relentless effort to get the job done.

Creating that sense of urgency first requires understanding that there is a performance challenge. And understanding the full nature of the performance challenge emerges from analyzing a wide range of performance data, often catalyzed by pressure to improve that emanates from many sources.

The chapter has three major sections. The first reviews the sources of pressure to improve performance that impacted these schools and districts. The second describes how most started analyzing state test data to fully understand their performance situation and to comprehend their performance challenge. The third describes the curriculum-mapping processes in which many of these education systems engaged.

1. PRESSURE TO IMPROVE PERFORMANCE

Pressure to improve performance emanates from several sources.

Pressure From NCLB

As the previous Odden and Archibald (2009) book showed, pressures to change are dropping on the American education system from multiple directions. For some it is the accountability press of the federal No Child Left Behind (NCLB) Act. With admitted (though I would argue not fatal) flaws,[1] NCLB is one education program that requires accountability for student performance. NCLB seeks to have all students make Adequate Yearly Progress (AYP) toward proficient achievement, and most important presses the system to reduce the multiple achievement gaps in student performance that characterize the student performance landscape in the United States. As more and more schools and districts fall short of the AYP goals as these shortcomings in performance are documented, districts and schools are put on notice that they have a performance challenge and many, though not all, respond by seeking to do better.

Many of the schools and districts referenced in this and other books (e.g., Chenoweth, 2007; Odden & Archibald, 2009)—the Columbus School in Appleton, Wisconsin; the Aldine School District just outside of Houston, Texas; and schools profiled by the Education Trust (see www.edtrust.org)—drew their initial inspiration to change from disappointment with their NCLB and AYP results.

Pressure From State Standards-Based Reforms

Before NCLB came to dominate the American education scene, states created their own versions of standards-based education reform, a change agenda that sought very similar student performance goals—high achievement for all students. As more state student testing flowed from these reforms, many districts began to assess the performance situation these data measured and, when the gap between desired and actual performance became clear, they set out to reduce that gap.

Pressure From the Business Community

Concurrently with both of these sources of performance pressure, the business community, along with most of the political communities across the country, began to demand higher levels of student knowledge and skill. The rationale for this pressure was the increasing linkage between economic growth and the skills of the workforce. Increasing numbers of jobs in the new economy, and those that provided high wages and were the growth engines of the new economy, required a broader and deeper range of student expertise. Again, as the nature of the skills gap between the worker skills needed by the new economy and the skills of students coming out of the education system became more well known, business and political leaders joined forces to pressure the education system to produce higher levels of student achievement, particularly for the rising number of students from low-income and minority backgrounds—who would become the majority of students in the near future.

Though some people questioned the motives of business involvement in schools, others showed that the skills needed by workers in the evolving, knowledge-based global economy were indeed much higher than were being produced by schools, and that low-skilled jobs were increasingly being exported to other countries (Friedman, 2005; Murnane & Levy, 1996). North Carolina's former governor and long-time education reform leader, James Hunt, began his focus on education back in the mid-1980s when he pledged to grow the North Carolina economy. He knew that a better education system was key to the economic growth of his state, and events since then have proven him correct.

Moral Drive to Improve Results

Others have been motivated by the "moral" drive to close the achievement gap and improve the performance of children from low-income and minority backgrounds. For example, when Jerry Weast became superintendent of the high-performing Montgomery County School District that borders our nation's capital, he showed the teachers, principals, and parents in that community that it was experiencing rapid demographic change and unless the district revamped the overall education system to address these altered circumstances, performance would likely drop and the moral challenge to educate all students to high performance levels would not be attained. As a result, he got the entire community to understand that it was a community in transition, and that regardless of demographics, it could not only maintain its high-performance reputation but also burnish it by educating its increasing numbers of low-income, minority, and immigrant students to the same high performance levels that had been attained mainly by its White, middle-class students in the past. And the district has done just that; its achievement gaps are very small, most subgroups have 90% or more of their students achieving at or above the Maryland proficiency levels, and the district has the most African American students taking and passing AP (advanced placement) exams than any other school district in the country, regardless of size.

Fullan (2008) and others have written about the "moral imperatives" of being a principal and "what is worth fighting for in the principalship," with the imperative being high levels of learning for all students, regardless of sociodemographic background. Many schools feel this internally generated pressure, and often their first step is to analyze their performance situation. Many of the examples of resource reallocation described in Odden and Archibald (2001b) began their restructuring efforts with this internally generated need to improve.

Pressure From Competition

Others argue for more competition in the school system as a strategy to create pressure for change. Policies that allow open student enrollment across district boundaries, charter schools, and even vouchers are often proposed as ways to pressure schools to improve performance, the notion being that competition for students would stimulate enhanced efforts to produce more student results.

In sum, the initial pressures to change emanate from many places. Though these pressures have not yet penetrated all districts and all schools, they nevertheless are present all over America and increasingly are pressing down on most school systems. In response, the first step many districts and schools take is to analyze existing performance data to understand the nature of their performance situation and thus their performance challenge.

2. ANALYZING STATE STUDENT TEST DATA

To gain an understanding of the current performance situation, all the schools and districts referenced in this book began by analyzing state student test data. The state testing data not only gave specific information on the overall status of student achievement but also gave information on achievement across different subgroups of students as well as across different subtopics of each content area tested. Urban districts, suburban, and rural districts engaged in this process, as did many districts with chronic achievement gaps between majority and minority populations.

Rural Districts

When Kennewick, Washington, a district of about 15,000 students in southeastern Washington, began its review of student performance data, the initial point was to have everyone in the school system as well as in the community simply understand that the district had a reading performance problem. The analyses showed that only about 57% of third-grade students scored at or above proficiency and the district concluded that was not good enough. The district set a goal of hiking that score to at least 90% in the short term—and pretty much attained that goal. In the initial process, each school not only identified the nature of learning gaps between majority and minority students but also identified shortcomings in performance by sub-skill areas. The result was that each school became quite familiar with the "texture" of their student achievement profiles, which helped them tailor responses to the conditions of their specific school—with all schools striving to teach at least 90% of all students, including the students from poverty backgrounds, to proficiency levels.

Monroe, in rural south-central Wisconsin, discovered that state tests showed its students did okay on basic skills in mathematics but did poorly on the problem-solving tasks. As a result, the district launched a major effort to change the mathematics curriculum in the district and adopted a textbook series that embedded problem solving throughout the school year; the goal was to improve both overall performance and performance in applying mathematics to problem-solving tasks.

Abbotsford, in north-central rural Wisconsin initially conducted a sociodemographic analysis. The process informed the broader community that as the local meat-packing plant doubled its size, the vast bulk of new workers came from Mexico, bringing into the schools increasing numbers of children who were not proficient in English. Knowing they would be held accountable for state test scores, the district restructured the reading curriculum to an approach tailored to English language learning (ELL) students, and the result was that even though the district experienced significant rising ELL enrollments, it increased the numbers reading at or above proficiency into the mid-90% range and doubled the portion of low-income students achieving at that level.

Urban Districts and Schools

Boston, New York City, and Chicago used the results from their state's student testing system to anchor their broad-based education improvement strategies. Chicago, the country's third largest district of 410,000 students with more than 85% low income, was not long ago called the "worst" school system in America. Boston's highly diverse district serves approximately 56,000 students, and New York City, the largest district in the United States, serves approximately 1,040,000 students. All three large, urban districts launched two parallel activities to improve student performance: One was an ambitious curriculum and instructional change effort, and the other was a series of initiatives to solve the staffing problems of their schools and to staff schools with talented principals and teachers with the goal of having no vacancies when school opened in the fall, including no vacancies for mathematics and science classes (see Archibald, 2008; Goertz & Levin, 2008; Kimball, 2008). The districts were successful on all fronts, and their scores on state tests doubled over a four- to six-year time period.

In Chattanooga, Tennessee, the low levels of student test scores in the schools in the poor section of that county school district were used to spawn the well-known Benwood Initiative, a partnership between a local foundation and the district to improve student test scores in those high-poverty, high-minority concentration schools (Chenoweth, 2007). These state test data showed that student performance in the Benwood schools was much lower than that of the schools in the more suburban part of the county and also was far below the state average. The state data further showed that students in the Benwood schools were over 80% African American and 95% were eligible for the federal free- and reduced-price program—in other words, students from families in poverty. The details of the overall reforms in this initiative have been chronicled elsewhere, but the result of those initiatives was that overall state test scores increased by over 50% for all the Benwood schools and doubled for many of them. Again, the public profiling of the poor results on the state tests were the catalyst for the launch of the reforms, and results from the same state testing system were used to show the fruits of the change efforts after only a five-year time period.

Dayton's Bluff School, a K–6 school with high concentrations of students from low-income and minority backgrounds in St. Paul, Minnesota, was dubbed one of the worst schools not only in St. Paul but in the entire state (Chenoweth, 2007). In 2000, state tests showed that nine out of ten students did not read on grade level. The school was in chaos. A new principal, a number of curriculum and instructional initiatives, very high expectations, and intensive professional development changed that performance profile so that by summer of 2007 nine of ten students did read on grade level, including over 90% of students from poverty backgrounds. The state tests were used to show that better performance was needed and then were used to show that better student performance had been attained.

Suburban Districts

Using state student testing data to identify more macrolevel weak areas in the curriculum and instructional programs represents one of the most useful aspects of this kind of data analysis. The Aldine School

District near Houston, a suburban district with urban demographics, in its 2008 presentation at the Doubling Student Performance Conference at the University of Wisconsin–Madison, argued that test score analysis does not provide solutions but does identify areas that need work (see the overview for Aldine, a 2009 finalist for the Broad Prize in Urban education www.broadprize.org). District leaders analyze the state testing results every year. In 2005, the district discovered a significant dip in science achievement. Upon further analysis, they discovered that their curriculum excluded several topics that were covered by the test. They not only added those topics into the next year's science curriculum but also provided professional development on the conceptual points for those units and monitored teachers to make sure the new units were taught; as a result, kids did better on the science test the next year. That year, the district also noted a drop in reading comprehension for Grade 5 English ELL students. They developed what they called a "layered" approach to reading and provided extensive training in how to implement that approach; Grade 5 ELL students did much better the next year. The district also used the overall district data to monitor student performance school by school, grade by grade, and classroom by classroom. Although the state testing data do not provide the detail for how to improve instructional practice, which is addressed by other elements of the district's overall instructional improvement strategies discussed throughout this book, they do identify the prime areas where achievement is not keeping pace with expectations, which allows the district to intervene in targeted ways by subject, topic within content area, grade level, and school.

Nagging Achievement Gap Districts

When Spokane, Washington, analyzed its state testing data, it faced a reality not expected. Though the district overall did relatively well, with about 65% or so of students achieving at or above the state proficiency level, it turned out that number was an average of much higher average achievement for the district's middle-class White students and much lower average achievement for the district's minority and lower-income students. This large achievement gap was a shock and an embarrassment, and the district decided to root out that performance inequity, and over the next five years made great strides in doing so (Fermanich et al., 2006).

Many other districts across the country have discovered that while the overall level of performance was fine, the district average was a combination of much higher performance for the White, middle-class students and much lower performance for their low-income and minority students, a situation that was not defendable. This is especially true of many districts in the Minority Student Achievement Network, a collaboration of districts, many high spending, often in large university towns (e.g., Madison, Wisconsin; Ann Arbor, Michigan; Evanston, Illinois; etc.), but with large achievement gaps between these groups of students. Madison, a member of this network, discovered in its analysis of state testing data that if students were below the basic level on the third-grade reading test, they never achieved beyond the basic level by the eighth grade; the district also knew that the bulk of students in the below-basic category were African Americans. The fact is that many districts are unaware of how large the gap is between minority and majority student achievement until a team sits down and actually analyzes the numbers. All districts in the Minority Achievement Network have pledged to eliminate their achievement gaps by raising the scores of their African American and low-income students; Madison explicitly sought to eliminate all students from the below-basic performance level.

In conclusion, nearly all schools and districts began their trek toward doubling performance by analyzing student test scores from the state testing program. Those scores described their beginning performance condition, and the goal in all places was to produce dramatic increases, if not double performance. I should add that none of the places studied spent much time criticizing the state tests or arguing that the tests assessed too narrow a version of achievement. The individuals may have had criticisms, and those criticisms may have been valid, but they all used the state tests as a *starting point* for understanding where they stood vis-à-vis student performance and used the results of the analysis to identify the macro areas where they needed to improve.

Don't Focus Primarily on Demographics

I also should note that most places we studied did not focus this analytic phase on student, family, or community demographics, in large part because they were not actionable on the part of schools.[2] They analyzed student performance data on the assumption that what schools did largely impacted student academic performance and that to improve performance a sophisticated understanding of the extant performance condition of the school and district was an essential first step.

On the other hand, there were some places that did analyze the demographic data but used the results to target what to improve on the expectations, curriculum, and instructional fronts and not to take the focus *off* of what the district could do to change student performance. The case of Montgomery County, a suburban district in Maryland, is a good example.

The district's demographic analysis, lead by Superintendent Jerry Weast, documented the changing nature of the demographics of the county, noting that what was subsequently termed the "red zone," which cut down the middle of that large district, was being increasingly populated by students from lower-income, minority, and immigrant families. Weast used the documentation as a rallying cry for the district to mount new strategies, stressing that these demographic realities required the district to maintain high expectations for these new students, and to mount a set of curriculum and instructional interventions to ensure that these students performed just as highly as the traditional students in the district.

Thus, in some cases, some demographic student analysis can be helpful, but only if it leads to conclusions about what the districts and schools can do to improve performance. This point is very important. Making the opposite point in a large state conference I attended in fall 2007, a leading educator gave the first keynote speech, noting how difficult it was to teach in urban systems. He gave the example of one of his students who was shot and killed during the school year, another who left school a drug addict and ended up in prison, and a third whose health declined so that he could not attend school. This was the kickoff keynote for a conference focused on reducing the achievement gap. But the symbolic message of this speech was clearly that schools and teachers could do little to overcome these traumatic and overpowering outside forces. Certainly that is true for the examples he gave.

But as stated in the preface to this book, education systems now enact policies and practices that reduce student performance: such as provide less funding to high-poverty districts and schools; assign the least-qualified, least-expert, and least-experienced teachers to the toughest students; skip "tough" curriculum topics in many classrooms; require student work in many high-poverty classrooms that reflects very low learning expectations; and otherwise do things that will reduce student performance. The districts that double performance focus on these things and target the implications of both their analyses of state testing data and student demographic data, when the latter are part of the overall initial analysis.

3. CONDUCTING CURRICULUM STANDARDS AUDITS

At this initial stage of data analysis, many of the schools and districts also engage in a curriculum-mapping process, comparing what content is included in their district and school content standards, what content is included in the state curriculum standards or frameworks, and what content is included on the state tests. In many cases, districts and schools discover that they are not teaching some of the content that is in the state curriculum standards and on the state tests. They also find that adding those units to the district and school curriculum is an "easy" first step change to make.

The Aldine example above is an excellent example of curriculum mapping that assessed the alignment of the state tests with the state and district curriculum content standards and with what teachers actually taught, and in turn modified the school and district curriculum to more closely align with the state curriculum standards and the scope of the state testing program. Though this process can very well lead to injecting complex new content into the local curriculum program, which needs to be followed by extensive and ongoing professional development, at the first level it is a relatively "easy" fix—teach all the curriculum content that is included in the state curriculum standards and that is covered by the state tests; otherwise student scores will be lower on the state test. To make sure students do well on the state tests, the new curriculum additions must be accompanied with effective professional development, but Step 1 nevertheless is to teach all topics that are covered in the state testing program.

In the Odden and Archibald (2009) book on resources for doubling performance, the district of Rosalia in rural Washington discovered that its curriculum gave writing short shrift and as a consequence, student writing scores on the state test were low. The first-step response was to teach more writing, and student scores on the state writing assessment rose immediately and dramatically.

4. SUMMARY

In sum, all schools and districts on the road to doubling student performance began by analyzing the student performance data provided by the state's testing system. They did not begin by saying they needed more money, they did not begin by criticizing the obvious flaws of the NCLB program, they did not begin by analyzing student demographics, and they did not begin by criticizing the state test or arguing that it measured a too-narrow aspect of student achievement. They began by analyzing data that measured the performance of their students. The goal was to understand the overall performance situation for their district and school, to see where students were performing well and where they were not, to understand differences in performance by student subgroups, and to understand how far or close their students' performance was to proficient and advanced levels of performance as indicated by state tests. It was a starting point.

And for many districts and schools, the findings were sobering. They discovered achievement gaps they didn't know existed, they learned that their performance was much lower than they had thought, they learned they were doing well on the basics but not on higher-order skills, and they learned they were doing fine in reading and mathematics but not other subjects. For these districts, the findings led to a call for dramatic action— actually, a set of actions described in the next chapters but that included dramatic restructuring of the school and reallocation of resources in many cases (Odden & Archibald, 2009).

NOTES

1. I need to say at the very beginning that NCLB has many flaws, that it is not a perfect law. But it has focused the entire education system on the issue of inadequate student performance, insufficient increases in student performance over time, and the continuing wide gap in performance between majority and minority students. It is this generic thrust of NCLB—to increase student performance and reduce the achievement gap—to which the above language refers.

2. This also is a point often made by the Education Trust; if the initial analysis focuses on demographics and family issues, the dilemma is that education systems cannot change those factors. So the analysis should be on performance in school, something the education system is well positioned to address.

Set Ambitious Goals

The second strategy in the process of doubling student performance is to set very high and ambitious goals, regardless of the current performance level or the nature of student demographics. As the reader will see, the goals set by the districts and schools doubling performance went way beyond just marginal improvements, or above "predicted value added," and even beyond what some might call "stretch" goals. For example, when a new person became principal of the Elmont Junior-Senior High School in suburban New York, he said the goal was to become one of the best high schools in the state. This was in response to a welcome to the school as one of the "best minority high schools" in the state; the new principal wanted the site to become not just a good school, not just one of the best high-minority schools, but with a student enrollment of 95% African American and a high percentage eligible for the federal free-and reduced-price lunch, one of the best schools in New York State—which has many high-performing schools. And the school met that goal.

The first section of this chapter notes how all these districts and schools went beyond what motivational theory would suggest for goal setting. Section 2 identifies the goals set by categories of districts: urban, suburban, rural, and schools in the 90-90-90 network. Section 3 argues that setting very ambitious goals is a hallmark of being an American.

1. BEYOND MOTIVATIONAL THEORY

Readers familiar with motivational theory will probably have read many articles about goal setting that suggest that goals, even stretch goals, should be reasonable and attainable. Goals need to be viewed by the workers in the organization as within their power and ability to attain. The idea is that good goal setting motivates individuals to focus their work on those goals and to channel their energies to attain them. Research shows that when goals are set too high, workers view goals as out of reach and unattainable, and do not work hard to attain them; as a result, the goals lose their motivating power. So implications from research on motivation would suggest some caution for schools' and districts' setting new goals for their students' achievement—set bold goals but make them reasonable.

As the goals identified in this chapter illuminate, however, the teachers, principals, and other leaders in the education systems referenced in this book must not have read that motivational literature. If they read it, they clearly did not abide by its policy recommendations because they set very, very high goals and, for the most part, attained them or came very close to attaining them.

Further, though there is much anguish around the country about the difficulty of achieving the AYP (adequate yearly progress) goals of the NCLB (No Child Left Behind) program, none of the schools and districts set AYP as their goal. Basically, AYP, even though seen by many as difficult to attain, represents a modest goal—to do a bit better next year than last year and to produce that progress for all student subgroups as well.[1] But we have studied several schools that did set AYP as their prime goal, and as a group, such schools did make progress but it was quite modest progress; such schools did not come close to *dramatically* improving performance, to say nothing of actually doubling performance.

To be sure, underneath the AYP goal is a desire to produce learning progress for all student subgroups and to reduce any achievement gaps; admittedly, this is the harder part of AYP. And goals to boost performance and close the achievement gaps carry with them some honor. But the goals set by the districts and schools that have doubled performance went far beyond just attaining AYP; they usually met AYP and produced gains for all subgroups, but their performance gains were much larger than just meeting AYP.

Finally, none of the schools and districts that doubled performance had a goal of just getting the "bubble" students over the proficiency bar. Although some research has documented this practice of focusing on the kids just below the proficiency standard in many schools and districts across the country, this practice reflects a very modest goal and does not lead to large, long-term student performance gains. It might produce one year of AYP, but the practices entailed in pushing the kids who are close to the proficiency bar just over it are inconsistent with the practices needed to sustain performance improvement over several years, and thus different from the practices needed to double student performance or educate 90 to 95% of students to a proficient or advanced level.

2. BEYOND THE SOFT BIGOTRY OF LOW EXPECTATIONS

Many of the districts and schools studied by my colleagues or others have high concentrations of students from poverty and minority backgrounds. Often in the past, expectations for these students succumbed to what some have called the "soft bigotry of low expectations." And of course, when performance expectations are low, even when attained do not represent large progress, and many students still end up not performing at proficient or otherwise adequate levels. At the same time, many districts and schools around the country have a hard time setting high goals when large portions of their students come from poverty backgrounds, minority ethnicities, or families who speak a primary language other than English. There is an often-implicit belief that such kids cannot learn to high standards.

One of the primary emphases of several of the districts in the Minority Student Achievement Network, mentioned in Chapter 1, has been to combat the racial aspect of this bigotry of low expectations. The network admitted to each other that as the demographics in their districts changed, many of the teachers and other leaders really did not believe that the rising numbers of low-income and minority children could achieve to high levels. As a result, expectations often were lowered for such students. Recall that most of the districts in the network are located in cities with large, nationally prominent universities. Many of the districts have stories of sons and daughters of minority professors—that is, sons and daughters of parents with doctorate degrees, being counseled out of advanced courses in high school, even though they had been earning As in previous classes. When the parents asked why, both guidance counselors and teachers said they did not think their children could handle the work. It was hard not to interpret this behavior as reflecting racial bias. And consequently, many of the districts have been working directly on that bias issue.

However, it should be clear that the people in the schools and districts that have doubled student performance and are the subject of the 10 strategies in this book not only believe that all children can learn to high levels, including children from poverty, minority, and non-English-speaking backgrounds; they also set high goals for the achievement and educated those students to those high levels of achievement. The people in these districts and schools were not befuddled by the demographics or characteristics of their students. They simply saw their job as educating students to high standards and set high goals for student performance, regardless of the sociodemographic conditions of their students, school, or community.

Two Examples

For example, the Aldine Independent School District near Houston, Texas, puts it this way:

> We believe every student can achieve at or above grade level and we will provide access to a quality education regardless of ethnicity, family income, gender, native language, special need, or area of residence. Further, we believe Aldine Independent School District can achieve higher levels of performance through clearly defined goals that set high expectations for student achievement.

This is a district that was 65% White in 1980. Today, this highly diverse district is made up of about 60,000 students from the following backgrounds:

- Approximately 30% African American
- 64% Hispanic
- 82% from poverty

And the district has met their goals:

- ☑ Over 90% of all students and all subgroups meet the state's Grade 3 reading standards.
- ☑ 86% of all students meet the state's Grade 5 reading standards with subgroup scores ranging from 79% for ELL students to 94% for White students.
- ☑ 95% of Grade 8 students meet the reading standards.
- ☑ More than 90% of all students and all subgroups meet the state's high school exit requirements.

The results are similar, though a bit lower, for mathematics and science. The point here is, this very diverse, large urban district believed all students can learn and set high expectations for all students, including all subgroups, which in turn produced the results for all students and all subgroups.

Long Beach, California, is another large, diverse, urban district that did the same thing. Long Beach School District borders Los Angeles and contains one of the largest ports in the United States. Long Beach School District's 88,000 students reflect the diversity of California:

- More than half (51%) are Hispanic.
- 18% are African American.
- 17% are White.
- 4% are Asian.
- 3.5% are Filipino.
- 5.5% are classified as "other."
- About two-thirds (68%) qualify for free- and reduced-price lunch, the typical education proxy for poverty.
- 24% are ELL and come from homes where one of 34 different languages is spoken.

The initial goals for improvement were for all third graders to read proficiently by the end of that grade and to eliminate social promotion by Grade 8. The district responded by not only doubling performance in the late 1990s and early 2000s, but also, when a new superintendent came on board, setting even more aggressive goals to build substantially on that progress. The new goals include a doubling of the number of students taking and passing AP (advanced placement) classes in high school without a decline in the AP passing rate, increasing the percentage of students taking algebra in Grade 8, and raising the number and percentage of students meeting the California requirements for entry into California public colleges and universities. And for the most part, the district has attained those goals (see the overview for Long Beach, a 2009 finalist for the Broad Prize in Urban education: www.broadprize.org).

Many districts have chosen to ignore the low expectations often associated with sociodemographic data of poverty and minority status, and instead, set high goals and met them. Further, the districts and schools breaking these socioeconomic status (SES) chains and setting high expectations represent small, medium, and large districts; and urban, suburban, and very rural districts. The population of large urban districts in this category is impressive:

- ☑ Boston tripled the performance of its students on the state math test over a five- to eight-year time period.
- ☑ Montgomery County Public Schools in Maryland, after conducting an analysis showing that the district was experiencing growth in the numbers of low-income, minority, and ELL students, set a goal to educate 100% of students to and beyond the state's proficiency standard, and the most recent state test results showed that the district has 90% of its very youngest children performing at or above state standards, including all key student subgroups.

And districts such as Atlanta; Santa Ana, California; and New York City have made large boosts in student academic performance, showing that it is possible to set and meet high goals for nearly all districts.

3. SETTING VERY HIGH GOALS

This section gives additional examples of the goals set by many different kinds of schools and districts. It is hoped that the various goals will serve as inspirations to other districts and schools discussing just how ambitiously they should determine their goals.

Before giving the examples of goal setting, it should be noted that oftentimes reviewing performance data with parents and the broader community can help encourage school systems to set very high and ambitious goals. Education systems often are reluctant to share performance data with parents and the local school community, especially when the results show low performance, fearing that public knowledge of these facts will lead to criticism of the school, which may or may not be warranted. However, several education systems have reported that the process of public disclosure of low performance can result in just the opposite—strong community encouragement to set very high goals (such as teaching all students to read) as well as strong community support for the changes, programs, and strategies required to attain the goal. These latter community supports were experienced by educators in Madison, Kennewick (Washington), Spokane, and the Teton School system in Wyoming.

Some Initially Modest Goals

We begin with what might now be viewed as a modest goal but that was a bold goal when initially set. The Madison and Kennewick districts set a goal of having 90% or more of students attain a proficient score on the state reading test by the end of third grade. When these goals were set during the late 1990s, they were considered quite ambitious. Both districts had growing numbers of students from low-income and minority backgrounds. Stating publicly that the goal was to get virtually all students to proficiency in reading by the end of third grade represented big, bold statements; they were part of what one could call a change in expectations that began to emerge across the country to set very high goals with the intention of attaining them. And both Madison and Kennewick have come very close to producing those results. As noted in Chapter 1, Madison accompanied that goal with a simultaneous goal of reducing to zero the number of students scoring at the below-basic level at the end of their grade, and also virtually attained that goal as well.

The rationale for the ambitious third-grade goal was the idea that children learn to read up to the third grade, and after that read to learn. If students could not read by the end of third grade, it would be very difficult for them to learn, not only in English but in all other subjects as well. Hence, these and other districts set a goal of getting every child to proficiency in reading by the end of grade three. This also was the thrust behind the federal Reading First program, which despite its problems, had meeting this goal as its primary task.

Madison actually set three overarching goals for the district:

- Have all students reading at or above proficiency by the end of Grade 3.
- Have all students take and pass algebra by the end of Grade 9.
- Have all students take and pass geometry by the end of Grade 10.

These goals guided the district for the next decade. These three goals—reading, algebra, and geometry—were considered "gateway" goals; if students could not meet them, they would have great difficulty exiting high school ready for college, ready for work in the global market, and ready for citizenship.

Urban District Goal Setting

Big urban districts have been setting ambitious goals. New York City was an example of a district that was performing far into the bottom half of all districts in the state. When the new mayor, Michael Bloomberg, and the new chancellor, Joel Klein, first took control of the schools, they set a two-part agenda. The first was to bring order to the organization, management, and performance of the district and produce adequate schools. That took three to four years. But then they set the goal of having the New York City District become outstanding and world class; the goal is not just to be a good urban district but one of the best in the country, if not the world. This also is the goal of the Chicago Public Schools—to become the best urban district in the country. And as we noted earlier, both of these districts have produced large gains in student performance, more than doubling performance in some subjects and some grade levels. Further, neither district is satisfied with the gains that have been made, and both want to take their districts to new levels—to be the best.

The Boston Superintendent, Carol Johnson, plans to build on Boston's substantial gains in the past decade by moving to an excellence agenda. The goals of this agenda are to have all students

- learn to read by the end of Grade 1
- read to learn by Grade 3
- be skillful and do analytic writing in Grade 7
- take algebra in Grade 8
- be on track to graduate by Grade 10
- have SAT I scores of 1,650+ points

These would be ambitious expectations for a suburban district; they are now the goals for the very diverse Boston Public Schools, which, like Long Beach, is building on the foundation of past performance gains to complete the next step in moving from good to great, or what New York City calls moving from adequate to outstanding.

The Spokane district in Washington State went beyond an ambitious goal for one subject and one grade level by making the goal to have 90% of students meeting standards in reading as well as mathematics, not only in Grade 4 but also in Grades 7 and 10. Indeed, using 2002 as the starting point, the district sought further to attain that goal, not in a generation, not in 10 years, but in 5 years, so to attain the goal by the end of the 2007 school year. To be sure, the goal created many conversations about the urgency to act boldly and professionally to attain the goal. And the district made huge progress toward accomplishing that ambitious set of goals.

What some might call audacious goals sometimes appear even more frequently when the focus is on individual schools. For example, the Capitol View Elementary School in Atlanta, Georgia, adopted the Core Knowledge program developed by E. D. Hirsch, on the notion that its students, nearly all African American and 80% eligible for free- and reduced-price lunch, needed high expectations and a classical education that most thought was more appropriate for schools in middle-class suburbs (Chenoweth, 2007). This is a "no excuse" school. Students study Greek, Egyptian, and Chinese history in addition to U.S. history. All students, all of whom are in Grades K–5, study French every day and they emphasize problem solving in mathematics. This aggressive program had staggering results:

- ☑ In 2005, 97% of all students met state proficiency standards in reading and 58% exceeded those standards.
- ☑ 80% of fifth graders exceeded state standards in reading.
- ☑ Math performance was a bit less outstanding, but 90% of all students met the state's math standards and 35% exceeded them.

These would be outstanding results for a suburban school; they are more than outstanding for this inner city, urban school that set very high expectations and met them.

Similarly, the Stanton Elementary School in Philadelphia (Chenoweth, 2007), an all-minority and nearly all-poverty school, set a goal of having the bulk of students achieve to the *advanced* level of performance. As its principal, Barbara Adderly said, "If you focus on advanced levels of performance, proficiency will take care of itself." As described in Odden and Archibald (2009), this goal of performing to the advanced standard also worked for the Monroe District in Wisconsin; by addressing performance shortcomings in areas that constituted advanced performance levels, the district not only boosted performance at the proficiency levels but more than doubled performance at the advanced levels. The goal for the all-poverty, all-minority urban elementary school in Philadelphia was probably a bit bolder than this goal for Monroe, but the point is that two very different education systems set goals to have their children perform at the advanced levels and made huge progress as a result.

The Victory School in Milwaukee, Wisconsin, profiled by Odden and Archibald (2009), also adopted this type of goal by incorporating into the school a curriculum for gifted and talented students, even though the bulk of their students were from lower-income and minority backgrounds; the school ignored demographics and set high expectations, and as the teachers and students worked hard on this curriculum, student test scores rose by large amounts in a short time period.

Rural District Goal Setting

As described in Chapter 1, Rosalia, in rural northwestern Washington, set a goal to have *all* of its students achieve to proficiency in reading and mathematics and be able to think analytically. That district, with a large concentration of ELL students, made great progress toward that set of objects, doubling performance in the process. The Abbotsford district in rural Wisconsin set a goal of having 90% of all students achieve at least to the proficiency level on state tests, and nearly attained this goal even though the percentages of low-income, immigrant, and ELL students rose every year.

Oakland Heights Elementary School is in a rural area about one hour west of Little Rock, Arkansas. An elementary school with a mixture of White, African American, and Latino students, about two-thirds of the students are eligible for the federal free- and reduced-price lunch program. The parents of most of the students work in the nearby Tyson chicken-processing plant or the ConAgra frozen-food plant. Students perform far above the Arkansas state average. Student proficiency in literacy rose from 41% in 2001 to 72% in 2006, and in mathematics from 48% to 89%, both representing large gains. But both teachers and the principal say that while significant progress is encouraging—and most schools would envy such progress—it is not enough, because the goal is to have all—100%—students meet the state's proficiency standards in reading and mathematics. Again, ambitious goals sustain the sense of urgency to keep on improving until the high goal is met; doubling performance isn't good enough because the goal of getting 100% of all students to proficiency in both reading and mathematics is the leading goal.

Suburban Goal Setting

As mentioned above, when the principal that began the process of improvement in Elmont Junior-Senior High School in suburban New York City first entered the school, the departing administrator said, "Welcome to one of the best minority high schools in the state of New York." The new principal decided to change that perception saying, "Why just a good minority high school? Let's make this one of the best overall high schools in the state."

With his school team, he set a goal of having all students pass all the New York State Regents tests, which are among the most rigorous end-of-course examinations in the country (Chenoweth, 2007). And when a few years ago, only 89% of the students did well on a Geography Regents test, the principal said, "We obviously got something wrong," and worked with the teachers in that department to modify the geography curriculum so that students would do much better the next year. Note that he did not say, "Well, this year's students weren't as smart as those in the past," a refrain often heard when scores drop for a grade level or subject area. The diagnosis was that the curriculum and instructional program had a problem that could be fixed, which would then lead to higher student performance the next year. The point: schools and districts that set high goals and do not meet them in one year do not blame the students; they take responsibility themselves, modify the curriculum program, and seek to reverse the drop the next year.

But Elmont had goals that went beyond just taking and passing the New York State Regents tests. Their goal is to have all students in the "advanced" Regents track, to have all students take at least one AP course, to have all students graduate, and to have all students attend college. The multiplicity of these high goals reinforce each other and help the school pretty much attain the goals, at least with 90%-plus of its students.

90-90-90 School Goals

Several schools with concentrations of children from low-income and minority backgrounds across the county have adopted what has been dubbed the 90-90-90 goal. The term, first articulated by Dr. Douglas Reeves, the founder and leader of the Leadership and Learning Center, in observing some high-performance schools in Milwaukee, refers to schools that have 90% of the students achieving to or above the state proficiency standard, and whose students are 90% or more eligible for free- and reduced-price lunch (again, a proxy variable for family poverty), and 90% or more from minority backgrounds. The 90-90-90 approach represents an ambitious goal and an ambitious goal for schools with large numbers and percentages of students who often do not achieve to high levels—children eligible for the free- and reduced-price lunch program and children from various minority backgrounds. Though Reeves would be the first to admit that good schooling and top instruction cannot overcome all the disadvantages that come with poverty, he also supports the enormous contributions that schools can make to the achievement of students from those backgrounds and the many 90-90-90 schools around the country are existence proofs of that belief.

4. THINKING BIG IS QUINTESSENTIALLY AMERICAN

Though this kind of big and bold thinking might seem irrational to some, others would argue that this is quintessentially American. Julie Kellor (2008), in an article in the *Chicago Tribune Magazine*, wrote about the American historian David McCullough. Kellor writes that for McCullough gumption is a word that sums up McCullough's view of the great Americans of whom he writes. McCullough writes about Americans who take on initiatives that make huge differences—Adams (forming a new, democratic country), Teddy Roosevelt (building the Panama Canal), John Roebling (the Brooklyn Bridge), and Truman (ending World War II). "He writes about Americans who work hard, dream big, and fall hard, and then get back up and try again . . . about Americans who possess guts and ambition and diligence. Lofty goals—and the down-to-earth perseverance to get the job done." Kellor continues that what intrigues McCullough is that these great countrymen, "Kept going. Kept trying. Kept pushing. Kept fighting. And that is what so entrances McCullough; not the impediments, not the daunting odds or the constant setbacks—and not even the golden triumphs. What impresses McCullough is the endless, valiant effort, the effort in the midst of chaos and despair." Finally, Kellor writes that McCullough is also disgusted with "this woe is me attitude, this idea that the stresses of our times are unprecedented." Such an attitude, McCullough argues, would not have formed a new democracy, won World War II, or built the Panama Canal.

Such an attitude would also not double student performance. If McCullough would write about those who do double performance, he would write about how they think big, dream the impossible, set a goal of accomplishing the task, and put in endless hours and valiant effort to get the job done despite the context of chaos and despair that describes the lives of many of the students in their schools.

Put simply, these big and bold goals set by the schools that double performance reflect the true spirit on which this country was built. Yes, the goals are audacious. But so is the fact that the leaders of the districts and schools that set them actually attain these goals through relentless work over several years.

5. SUMMARY

The point here is threefold. First, all the districts and schools that have doubled performance set *very* high goals; they strive for "quantum improvements" in performance, not just marginal improvements. To many educators, these goals might seem unattainable, but they are set very high nevertheless, and the schools believed they could be attained.

Second, the goals apply to *all* students, including low-income and minority students. Schools and districts doubling performance seek to break the confinements of student demographics; they do not want to be seen as the best poverty school or the best minority school, but as a top school period, regardless of the demographic composition of their student body.

Third, even if the schools and districts did not attain their ambitious goals, they make huge progress toward their goals and thus are in a much better place than when they started. If the goal is to have 90% of all low-income and minority students achieve to or above proficiency, from a position of, say, 30% today, having 85% at that level after a five-year period of hard work would not be considered a failure. Although the specific goal of 90% might not have been reached, boosting proficiency performance from the 30% level to the 85% level represents a huge and significant improvement.

After understanding the complexities of the current status of student performance in their school or districts, the places that doubled performance set very high goals for the future—getting all students up to or beyond a proficiency bar, focusing on educating a large portion of students to the advanced level of performance, or having all students pass end-of-course examinations or graduate from high school. In a very real sense, these goals are more than just stretch goals; they are ambitious goals that in most cases neutral observers would say could not be met. But as the cases we and others (e.g., Chenoweth, 2007) have studied, the goals were met by these districts and schools.

Further, the teachers, principals, and district administrators leading these systems are not satisfied with the large gains they have made. In writings and presentations, they document the progress, say they are proud of the gains that have been made, and state that they have significantly more progress to make. In New York City, this is stated as moving from adequate to outstanding. In Oakland Heights, it was stated as wanting all students to perform to proficiency in reading and mathematics. In Long Beach, it took the form of ratcheting up the expectations at the high school level for AP course taking, eligibility for the stiff entrance requirements of the University of California and California State University systems, and college attendance rates. At Capitol View Elementary it took the form of the classical curriculum that is part of the Core Knowledge program.

Moreover, getting to "good" simply provides the foundation for moving to "great." And these ambitions permeate schools with high concentrations of low-income and minority students. The people leading these educational organizations break the chains of the bigotry of low expectations, and when they improve dramatically, they set aspirations even higher. They want their districts, schools, and students to be among the best. They believe they can attain those goals, and they work smartly, professionally, and relentlessly to attain them. They are ambitiously successful and successfully ambitious. And they will say, they are just ordinary educators determined to do an extraordinary job—implying if they can do it, others can also do it too, and if they don't, it is because of lack of interest and will, not money, students, or demography.

Last, in setting high goals, many of the districts and schools involved the community in the process. As a result, they had community understanding that the district/school had a performance issue, community support for setting high goals and community acknowledgement that the aspirations were ambitious, and community support for the school/district's engaging in the new types of strategies required to boost performance, including funding and reallocation of funding in many instances.

NOTES

1. I realize I am understating the task of meeting AYP goals for many schools, especially those that have students in many different demographic categories; failure to produce sufficient learning gains in any one cell means the school or district "fails" to meet AYP that year. Further, when states set achievement goals as a "step" function, in the year that all goals are ratcheted up to the next performance "step," schools are asked to make very large, rather than marginal, improvements and often fail to do so. My comment refers to AYP systems that require just small marginal gains each year. The double-performing schools and districts simply set much higher absolute goals.

Change the Curriculum Program and Create a New Instructional Vision

S trategy 3 addresses the core educational issues that educators in schools can change—the curriculum and the instructional program, which are the driving engines of all educational programs. Schools and districts that produce high levels of student performance focus on what they can affect, which is everything that happens in schools: the assignment of teachers, academic expectations, the organization of curriculum and instruction, the curriculum program and textbooks, and effective instructional practice. They do not focus on things they cannot change, such as family poverty, the lack of health care for many urban children, problems with parent involvement, full funding of NCLB (No Child Left Behind), the shortcomings with the state testing system, the accountability glitches of NCLB, and so on. They address the pieces of the education system over which they have control—the largest being the curriculum and instructional programs. And that allows them to act.

This was true for all the schools and districts studied. Using the language of the large-scale educational-change process (Odden & Archibald, 2009),

Strategy 3 entails framing a new educational vision for the district/school, a vision that for most districts/schools included a complete redesign of their curriculum and instructional program.

To make the point bluntly, the schools threw out their old curriculum programs and either bought or created new curriculum programs. Over time they also developed a view of effective instructional practice that fit with the new curriculum and that all teachers were expected to use in their classrooms (and that became the focus of professional development as well).

Thus the first section describes some of the new textbook series adopted by many of these systems, and their rationales for calling them "research based." This section also describes several points of view about effective instructional practice developed by various districts. Section 2 provides some caveats about claims for all the curriculum and instructional decisions being research based and refers the reader to sources that have conducted reviews of evidence on various curriculum programs and instructional strategies. Section 3 makes the point that all this work was conducted in a collaborative fashion by teachers and administrators.

1. ADOPTING NEW TEXTBOOKS AND INSTRUCTIONAL VISIONS

Districts and schools across the country adopted a wide variety of textbook series and views of effective instructional practice.

A New Approach to Reading

Districts and schools took different approaches to improving the reading program. Examples are given for Kennewick, Washington; Madison, Wisconsin; and Richmond, Virginia.

Kennewick, Washington. Nine of the thirteen elementary schools in Kennewick adopted the *Open Court Reading program.* According to the principal of the most-improved elementary school in the district—Washington Elementary School's Dave Montague—*Open Court* starts with phonemic awareness, moves to phonetics and then quickly to comprehension, and has an extensive array of classroom exercises and supplementary materials. *Open Court Reading* has been adopted by many schools and districts across the country, particularly urban districts.

According to the What Works Clearinghouse that has been reviewing reading programs, *Open Court Reading* is an elementary basal reading program for Grades K–6 developed by SRA/McGraw-Hill.[1] The program is designed to systematically teach decoding, comprehension, inquiry and investigation, and writing in a logical progression. Part 1 of each unit, "Preparing to Read," focuses on phonemic awareness, sounds and letters, phonics, fluency, and word knowledge. Part 2 of each unit, "Reading and Responding," emphasizes reading for understanding with literature, comprehension, inquiry, and practical reading applications. Part 3 of each unit, "Language Arts," focuses on communication skills such as spelling and vocabulary, writing process strategies, English language conventions (such as grammar, speaking, and penmanship), and basic computer skills.

The *Open Court Reading* program has been adopted across the country by many schools and districts that have concluded that a more structured approach to reading is needed for their children. This approach should include the emphasis on phonemic awareness for very young elementary school children, be followed by phonics, and also reach the comprehension stage because comprehension is the goal of fluent reading.

Over a 10-year time period, this reading program worked very well for Kennewick. In 1996, only 57% of its third-grade students read at the proficiency level on the rigorous state reading test; that number reached 90% in 2006. Today the portion of third-grade students in that district who read at or above grade level hovers just below and just above 90%.

Madison, Wisconsin. As indicated in previous chapters, through analysis of state testing data, Madison discovered it had a significant reading achievement gap and set a goal of eliminating that gap. During that initial data analysis, it also discovered that there was no reading program in the district—reading strategies and reading textbooks not only varied across all elementary schools but also varied significantly across classrooms in each elementary school. The district concluded that such a disjointed approach to reading instruction would not work for its increasingly diverse and more mobile student population. But this was a district that historically had let each teacher choose not only the curriculum to teach but how to teach it. Because of this, new central-office edicts would not work even though system change was needed.

Thus rather than adopting a particular textbook series, Madison created its own "balanced" reading program that stressed a balance of reading comprehension, writing, and phonics. Using a bottom-up approach that mirrored the Madison culture for making change, a group of central-office experts, principals, and teachers recognized for their reading expertise, created a new, districtwide, research-based reading program over a multiple-year time period. In the first year, they created a short document on the nine elements of a good reading program—phonemic awareness, phonics, vocabulary, comprehension, writing, and so on. Teachers then asked for more detail. The document was expanded the next year, and even more detail was then requested. By the end of the process, a document of more than 100 pages was produced, providing explicit guidance for reading strategies that helped teachers design instructional programs for each week of the school year.

During this same time period, the committee also developed a document that teachers used for formative assessments, collecting a "running record" of where each individual student was on various reading goals and objectives. The results of these running records were then discussed in groups to determine the kinds of reading instructional strategies the data implied for the nine different areas of reading instruction. Further, a copy of all running records was sent to the central office, where a staff person reviewed them all. That staff member then would visit the school and have discussions with the principal and teachers about specific students who were not making progress, asking questions about why, what the teacher was doing to help the student progress, and if the district could do anything to help the school move those students forward in reading proficiency.

Richmond, Virginia. Richmond, Virginia is another urban district that has produced huge gains in elementary reading scores. It accomplished these results initially by using a scientifically based reading program called Voyager and then shifted to the Houghton Mifflin Reading Series. The district concluded that both programs reflected the approach to the five components of effective reading instruction suggested by the National Reading Panel:

1. Phonemic awareness (identifying and being able to make the sounds in words)

2. Phonics (understanding how letters are linked to sounds)

3. Fluency (reading orally with speed and accuracy)

4. Vocabulary (understanding the meaning of words)

5. Comprehension (understanding the meaning of whole passages of text)

The district initiated these changes to bring consistency to reading after it found that across its many schools there was no district reading program; indeed, it found that there were over 29 different reading programs, which varied not only across schools but also across grades within individual schools. This dramatically varying approach to reading instruction was not working for Richmond's increasing numbers of low-income, minority, and mobile students. Using a consistent approach to reading, along with formative assessments linked to that curriculum, which helped teachers understand what students did and did not know for the unit being taught, the district boosted student reading proficiency as indicated in Table 3.1.

Table 3.1 Richmond, Virginia, Boost in Student Reading Achievement (Percentage At or Above Proficiency)

Year	2002	2008	% Point Change
Grade 3	45	75	30
Grade 5	53	80	27

Source: Dubin (2008).

A New Approach to Mathematics

Some schools and districts focused initially on the mathematics program. Examples are taken from Monroe and LaCrosse, both in Wisconsin.

Monroe, Wisconsin. The Monroe district in rural Wisconsin adopted a research-based and commercially available mathematics program, *Everyday Mathematics*, which several other elementary schools around the country have also adopted.

Everyday Mathematics is supported by the University of Chicago School Mathematics Project, a National Science Foundation-funded center established to support educators, parents, and students who are using *Everyday Mathematics*. *Everyday Mathematics* is a comprehensive prekindergarten through sixth-grade mathematics curriculum developed by the University of Chicago School Mathematics Project and published by Wright Group McGraw-Hill. Over 175,000 classrooms around the country enrolling 2.8 million students are currently using this textbook, and it is being adopted by a steadily increasing number of schools each year. The Web site http://everydaymath.uchicago.edu/about/curriculum has been created as a resource for the growing number of *Everyday Mathematics* users. According to the Web site, a number of features distinguish the *Everyday Mathematics* curriculum:

Real-life problem solving: *Everyday Mathematics* emphasizes the application of mathematics to real world situations. Numbers, skills, and mathematical concepts are not presented in isolation, but are linked to situations and contexts that are relevant to everyday lives. The curriculum also provides numerous suggestions for incorporating mathematics into daily classroom routines and other subject areas.

Balanced instruction: Each *Everyday Mathematics* lesson includes time for whole-group instruction as well as small group, partner, or individual activities. These activities balance teacher-directed instruction with opportunities for open-ended, hands-on explorations, long-term projects and on-going practice.

Multiple methods for basic skills practice: *Everyday Mathematics* provides numerous methods for basic skills practice and review. These include written and choral fact drills, mental math routines, practice with fact triangles (flash cards of fact families), daily sets of review problems called Math Boxes, homework, timed tests, and a wide variety of math games.

Emphasis on communication: Throughout the *Everyday Mathematics* curriculum students are encouraged to explain and discuss their mathematical thinking, in their own words. Opportunities to verbalize their thoughts and strategies give children the chance to clarify their thinking and gain insights from others.

Enhanced home/school partnerships: Daily Home Links (Grades K–3) and Study Links (Grades 4–6) provide opportunities for family members to participate in the students' mathematical learning. Study Links are provided for most lessons in Grades 4–6, and all grades include periodic letters to help keep parents informed about their children's experience with *Everyday Mathematics.*

Appropriate use of technology: *Everyday Mathematics* teaches students how to use technology appropriately. The curriculum includes many activities in which learning is extended and enhanced through the use of calculators. At the same time, all activities intended to reinforce basic computation skills are clearly marked with a "no calculator" sign.

Finally, the scope of the K–6 *Everyday Mathematics* curriculum includes the following mathematical strands:

- Algebra and Uses of Variables
- Data and Chance
- Geometry and Spatial Sense
- Measures and Measurement
- Numeration and Order
- Patterns, Functions, and Sequences
- Operations
- Reference Frames

As noted previously, after Monroe implemented this new mathematics program, student performance not only rose on the state's proficiency scale, but student performance doubled on the advanced scale of mathematics performance, a level that measured the ability to use mathematical concepts in a variety of problem-solving contexts.

LaCrosse, Wisconsin. Franklin Elementary in LaCrosse adopted *Investigation Mathematics.* Published by Scott Foresman (since bought by Pearson), *Investigations Mathematics* (http://investigations.scottforesman.com)

> offers activity-based mathematics that encourage students to think creatively, develop *and articulate* their own problem-solving strategies, and work cooperatively with their classmates. Many *Investigations* activities involve engaging games that reinforce students' understanding of important mathematical concepts and skills. The curriculum at each grade level is organized into units that offer from three to eight weeks of mathematical work in number, data analysis, and geometry. These units link together to form a complete K–5 curriculum that teachers can adjust to meet their classroom needs. Active mathematics teaching requires teachers to think deeply about the mathematics content their students are learning and the instructional techniques that meet diverse needs and learning styles.

Ongoing assessment opportunities in *Investigations* give teachers an overall picture of how their entire class is doing on a particular topic. They help teachers make decisions about modifying the curriculum. And in tandem with end-of-unit assessments, they allow teachers to evaluate each student's understanding and document his or her growth over time.

Investigations Mathematics emerged from a National Science Foundation-funded project to create a research-based elementary mathematics curriculum initially called TERC Math. And the program worked very well for this school. For all students as a group, scores of Franklin Elementary students on the Wisconsin testing system went from 23% proficient in 2002 to 77% proficient in 2005, more than tripling over that short time period. There was also impressive growth in the percentage of students who scored at the advanced level in mathematics during that time period, rising from only 10% of students in 2002 to 31% in 2005—again, a tripling of scores.

A High School Approach

Because Elmont Junior-Senior High School wanted all students to take and pass New York State's rigorous, curriculum-based Regents tests, the school threw out all former remedial and general education courses and included only courses aligned with the New York Regents exams. The theory was that to become the best high school in the state all students should be required to take a college preparatory academic program that was aligned with the state's end-of-course testing program called the New York State Regents Tests. Student scores on those tests assessed the effectiveness of the courses of study, which each department worked collegially to create and which each teacher used; as noted earlier, if student performance dropped, the department collectively analyzed those test scores and modified the curriculum to strengthen the area where student performance was the weakest.

Moreover, Elmont believed that the only way to produce the student achievement results was through high-quality instructional practice, and it organized the school to ensure that all teachers learned and deployed in their classrooms the instructional strategies that were collaboratively developed by department teams in all academic departments. The core of each unit was a series of lesson plans that were carefully developed and that each teacher was to use in teaching the unit. Every summer, department faculty analyze student scores on the Regents test for the course and where weaknesses are noted change both the curriculum unit itself and the specific lesson plans that comprised it. To ensure fidelity of lesson-plan implementation, every teacher receives six announced classroom observations every year—a three-day continuous observation by the department chair, a one-day observation by the chair, and then a one-period observation by the principal and one by the assistant principal. Moreover, when the principal conducts the observation, he reads all previous observations to learn what growth and change objectives had been set for the teacher and notes whether the instructional practice observed reflected those changes.

A Point of View About Good Instructional Practice

In addition to or instead of focusing on just one or two content areas, other districts developed a "point of view" about effective instructional practice it wanted all teachers to use. Examples are drawn from Kennewick; Aldine, Texas; Montgomery County, Maryland; and Long Beach, California.

Kennewick, Washington

Though Kennewick believed that good curriculum materials, such as the *Open Court* reading textbook series, are very important, the district also created a more specific view of effective reading instructional or pedagogical practice that it wanted used in delivering the *Open Court* or any selected reading curriculum program. In fact, both district leaders and the principals of the most-improving schools argue that good instruction is the way teachers put all the strategies of the school into practice to produce student achievement results. As one administrator put it, "Quality instruction isn't just everything, it is the only thing." Though this somewhat overstates the case, as there are other elements to the district's overall education improvement strategy, the quote emphasizes the importance the district attaches to instructional quality and one reason why the district developed an explicit view of what good reading instruction would entail.

Kennewick defined its point of view of good reading instruction as PERR, saying that all lessons need to have *purpose, engagement, rigor,* and *results.*

By *purpose* the district means that the teacher intentionally plans instruction focused on a learning that is linked to the district's core student learning goals. By *engagement* the district means that teachers must engage students in the learning process for each lesson taught. *Rigor* means that lessons must cover all aspects of the district's curriculum, including excellent reading comprehension and writing. And by *results* the district means that the effectiveness of each teacher's instructional practice will be assessed by its impact on student learning.

Each lesson's purpose is to be clearly communicated to students (such as by writing it on the blackboard), referenced consistently throughout the lesson and instructional unit, and connected to previous learning in a manner that over time develops all the knowledge and skills needed by the student to be a competent reader.

The purpose of the lesson is even more basic to each lesson plan than the previous paragraph suggests. Teachers are encouraged to write the purpose of the lesson on the board, and then state the purpose at the beginning of the lesson. Teachers are also asked to show principals (and during the lesson even show students) how students will demonstrate that they have learned the purpose of the lesson. Lessons also are designed to have students "discover" the purpose as the lesson proceeds. Thus, for each lesson taught, students are explicitly informed about what they are supposed to learn, are required to write the purpose as an "I" statement such as "I will summarize my analytic points in a closing paragraph," and are finally required to apply the learning of the lesson in a way that shows whether they have learned the purpose of the lesson.

This approach to lesson planning is also reinforced by several supervisory activities. Each central-office person who engages in reading supervision is assigned to work with three principals in different schools. When the central-office staff comes to the school, he or she, together with the principal, does "learning walks." All central-office individuals as well as all principals are required to do such learning walks in classrooms at least two hours every day, or ten hours every week, including the post-walk-through conference. During the learning walks, both the central-office supervisor and the principal look for purpose, engagement, rigor, and reflection in the reading lessons being used. The questions they have in their mind as they observe lessons are these: (1) What was the purpose of the lesson? (2) Was the purpose communicated to students? (3) Did the instruction match the purpose? (4) Did the students know the purpose? And during the after-walk discussion, the team asks the teacher what evidence he or she has to determine whether the purpose of the lesson was met, what questions the teacher has that will help to make that lesson better the next time it is used, and to organize the next units or lessons of instruction.

Further, teachers also are actively encouraged to watch other teachers' instructional practice. As they watch, they are encouraged to ask themselves several questions:

- What am I trying to learn?
- How did the teacher communicate purpose to students?
- How did the teacher collect data to know whether the purpose was attained and that students learned the purpose of the lesson?
- How can I use such strategies in my own instructional repertoire?
- What additional supports would I need to do that?
- What further questions do I have about the instructional episode I watched?

Kennewick has not only developed a point of view about what good reading instructional practice looks like; it also provides professional development that helps teachers learn how to engage in that instructional approach, including observing other expert teachers. It reinforces that instructional vision with central-office and principal strategies for supervising teachers (the learning walks) by focusing explicitly on how the teacher is implementing that instructional approach and by providing feedback in the post-learning-walk conference, which is designed to help the teacher improve instructional practice if shortcomings are noted during the walk.

From this description it should be clear that it is not a teacher's choice as to whether to implement the district's point of view about effective reading instructional practice. All teachers are expected to implement that instructional approach. And supervision of both teachers and principals is structured to help teachers perfect that instructional practice in their classrooms both by training principals in how to conduct learning walks to get data that can be used to help teachers improve their instructional practice, and by actually having the learning walks conducted constantly throughout the school year so that teachers periodically are being observed and engage in reflective conversations about their instructional practice and its impact in getting students to learn how to read.

Aldine, Texas

Aldine, a district with about 66,000 students, most of whom are from minority and low-income family backgrounds, is a suburban district with urban characteristics located right next to Houston International Airport on the north side of Houston. This district began its development of a point of view about quality instruction by first training principals and instructional leaders in what to look for during classroom observations, and followed this training with professional development for teachers. The district's goal was to have everyone learn how to use effective instructional strategies—summarizing, automaticity, word wall, KWL (K = what I already know, W = what I want to learn, L = what I learned), manipulation, organizing data, KWL extension, word wall extension (classify/categorize), visual verbal word association, problem solving—and to ensure fidelity of implementation by equipping principals and instructional coaches with the skills to monitor teacher performance according to this instructional system.

As this district view toward instructional practice became implemented, the goal was for all teachers, at all levels and in all subjects, to use these strategies in their instructional practice. Initially, some teachers, particularly high school teachers, pushed back. But principals were encouraged to evaluate—both through formal evaluations and more informal walk-throughs—all teachers on the basis of their using the strategies, pushing all teachers for fidelity to these district-sanctioned instructional practices. Since principals were first trained in how to observe and discuss these instructional strategies, they were able to execute the district's press for this approach to instruction. Further, when most teachers actually tried these instructional practices, they found that they were indeed helpful in increasing student achievement. Teachers' commitment to the instructional system evolved over time as they acquired the practices, used them in their classrooms, and experienced good student achievement results.

Over time, the district added more complex strategies such as inclusion of children with disabilities, expanding the overall approach to what is called "response to intervention," incorporating a district approach to discipline, and ensuring alignment of the curriculum that teachers taught with that of the state's curriculum standards for students.

In short, Aldine not only has its own written curriculum; it also seeks to have all teachers implement that curriculum with the Aldine model of effective instructional practice. All new teachers are given training in this approach to instruction. And the district—through professional development, new teacher induction with mentors, school-based instructional coaches, and ongoing formal and informal teacher evaluations by principals regarding this approach to instruction—seeks to have a consistent approach to instructional practice across all schools, classrooms, and subject areas.

Moreover, the district has recently created a Web-based system called TRIAND, designed to help all teachers implement its approach to instruction with examples of lessons, test items, and video clips linked to the district's content standards. The sample lesson plans are quite detailed with many specifics for how to teach the lesson and are often accompanied by video clips of teachers actually implementing that lesson plan. The system has been especially helpful to new teachers who, like those in Montgomery County discussed below, have many examples of how to teach their subject or grade-level curriculum; new teachers are not left to fend for themselves, but can draw from the expertise of more senior teachers with the materials in the Web-based TRIAND system.

Last, Aldine has developed a clear inclusion approach to working with students who are struggling and who might also have a specific disability. First, all students receive instruction in the core curriculum. And the performance of all students is monitored for each curriculum unit. Second, if the student is struggling, teachers are trained to provide appropriate accommodations, which could be putting a student into a reading group, providing a student with a multiplication chart, and things of this nature—the point being that this initial extra help is provided by the regular classroom teachers. The next step of extra help is having an additional teacher enter the regular classroom and provide certain students, or groups of students, some degree of extra help; this step can range from simple extra help to a coteaching approach where the regular teacher and the specialist teacher plan together and provide for a variety of different student needs in the regular classroom. This is followed by pull-out tutoring and then resource or self-contained approaches to instruction. Again, all teachers are trained in this district approach to inclusion.

In short, there are three tiers of special attention provided in the regular classroom before a student is referred for additional services because of a disability:

- Tier 1 provides quality classroom instruction for all students in the regular classroom, using data to target student needs. This is sufficient for 75 to 90% of all students.
- Tier 2 provides supplemental instruction in small, flexible, homogeneous groups within the regular classroom, not every day but up to two or three times a week. This is needed for 10 to 25% of students.
- Tier 3 provides specific individual intensive intervention provided every day, which could include individual or small-group tutoring. This is need for 2 to 10% of students.

It is only when all these efforts are not fully successful in helping the student achieve standards that there would be referral for special education. Finally, all these interventions are provided by licensed district staff.

Aldine calls this a managed approach to instructional practice, or managed instruction. Though there is significant teacher input into the development of the system, it is an instructional system, and all teachers in the district are expected to implement all of its parts, with fidelity ensured by formal and informal monitoring of teacher practice by principals, and with principals being held accountable for this monitoring.

Montgomery County, Maryland

Montgomery County Public Schools offers yet a different approach to how a common curriculum and common approach to instruction was developed across all grade levels and all subjects in the districts. Over several years, the district first developed a set of detail-of-curriculum standards that were aligned with the rigorous Maryland curriculum standards. The Montgomery County standards specified the scope and sequence of the curriculum that was to be taught to all students in the district. For example, the district identified the nature of calculus that was to be taught in Grade 12. Then it backward mapped down through each lower grade in the system identifying the mathematics that should be taught, and producing such content standards even for their preschool programs.

Next, the district encouraged teams of teachers, both across schools and within schools, to develop formative assessments to use in teaching that curriculum, as well as common end-of-curriculum unit tests. Within schools, common lesson plans and approaches to teaching each curriculum unit were developed. The bulk of the materials for every curriculum unit was teacher developed. Then all teachers would teach the collaboratively developed units, after which they would meet in groups within schools to assess the student performance results across all classes that were taught that unit. In this way, the teachers could see which strategies worked the best, which teachers were producing the most and the least student performance, and how to provide teacher-specific assistance so that all teachers could become more effective.

The point here is that the formative assessments, the curriculum units, and the common end-of-unit assessments were all teacher developed—the district did not buy them from a commercial textbook or curriculum provider. And as noted earlier, the performance of Montgomery County's students, including its low-income and minority students, is very high.

Long Beach, California

Long Beach made the foundation of its first round of reform an explicit view of instructional practice that could be used for all subjects and pretty much all grade levels (Koppich, 2008). The core of the district's instructional improvement strategy was the Essential Elements of Instruction. Based on the work of Madeleine Hunter, the Essential Elements revolve around the belief that teaching is a constant stream of teacher decisions structured around a set of "principles of learning" that guide teachers' decision-making processes and instructional actions. Using these principles, teachers establish an objective for each lesson, teach the lesson, and correct for students' level of understanding, using diagnostics and assessments. Effective teachers use strategies that help ensure that students are constantly engaged in what they are learning (called "active participation") and facilitate students' employing their past experiences to relate to the current lesson (called "anticipatory sets"). Motivation, closure, and reinforcement are also part of the Essential Elements of Instruction. Though this approach emerged during the 1970s and 1980s, when the emphasis across the country was on basic skills, it is a framework that can be readily used in teaching higher-order and problem-solving skills as well.

Long Beach adopted the Essential Elements approach to instruction across the district on the initiative of the superintendent at that time, Carl Cohn. After completing several "listening tours" with school principals around the district, at the same time knowing that the district was hiring 600 to 800 new teachers a year, it was clear to Cohn that there was no consistent approach to instruction in the district. Most of the novice teachers came to the district from a wide variety of teacher-preparation programs, each with its own view of good instruction. Cohn became convinced that these and all teachers in the district needed to speak a common language around lesson planning and the fundamentals of teaching, and thus adopted the Essential Elements of Instruction.

Over time, the Essential Elements became part and parcel of what Long Beach did instructionally. This approach to instruction ultimately infused the preparation of almost all new teachers, most of whom now receive their preservice training from California State University Long Beach, where Long Beach senior teachers serve as the supervising teachers for those individuals' student-teaching experiences. That approach to instruction shapes the interviews for new hires, as well as the district-run teacher induction program, and ongoing professional development.

An Approach Geared to a Specific Population

Because of its increasing number of English language learning (ELL) students and the goal to have all students learn to high standards while restructuring the entire school Columbus Elementary in Appleton, Wisconsin, selected the schoolwide *Different Ways of Knowing* program, a comprehensive school design and a product of the Galef Institute that had proven to be successful with students who were ELL.

Several schools profiled in my earlier book on restructuring and resource reallocation also selected comprehensive school designs, including *Success for All*, the *Modern Red Schoolhouse, Expedition Learning/Outward Bound*, and *Core Knowledge* (Odden & Archibald, 2001b). *Success for All* includes a structured approach to reading, with a heavy focus on phonics, but also emphasizes writing and reading comprehension. The *Modern Red Schoolhouse* uses a classical curriculum developed by E. D. Hirsch (1999a, 1999b, 1999c). *Expedition Learning* embraces a project approach to curriculum and includes expeditions out into the broader community for nearly all curriculum units as part of its program. Each comprehensive school design has a particular approach not only to curriculum but also a particular approach to the instructional strategies used to teach that curriculum.

The concept behind these types of curriculum changes is similar: Schools or districts choose what new, research-based strategy that, in their view, fits the particular needs of its students and that they believe will help them attain the high student achievement goals set for their students.

2. ASSESSING EFFECTIVENESS OF CURRICULUM AND INSTRUCTIONAL APPROACHES

The theme for Strategy 3 is adopting a new curriculum program in all content areas, but particularly reading and mathematics, and implementing it with an aligned instructional approach tailored to that program and sanctioned by the district. As the examples indicate, districts and schools took quite different approaches to these tasks, calling them research based in most instances.

I am not in a position to assess the correctness or rigor of all the programs selected, or the specific approaches to instructional practices, even though they helped the districts and schools to produce large gains in student performance. Nevertheless, it cannot be said with a technical certainty that all of the programs were research based, though many of the individuals in the schools made that claim.

Thus, readers are encouraged to review data in the Best Evidence Encyclopedia (BEE: www.bestevidence.org) that provides research-based reviews of reading and math programs for elementary, middle, and high schools, reading programs for ELL students, and many comprehensive school reform designs. Readers are also encouraged to visit the information in the federally supported What Works Clearinghouse (http://ies.ed .gov/ncee/wwc), which reviews evidence on textbook series, as well as many other educational interventions (such as class-size reduction). These are two Web sites that provide a range of evidence and advice on what programs research has proven to be effective. The only caveat to this suggestion is that the standards the What Works Clearinghouse use for good evidence are so stringent that very few programs of any sort have "good" evidence on their impact. Nevertheless, both sources provide additional information on the effectiveness of various curriculum programs, textbook series, and other educational actions.

Readers also are invited to follow the research summaries published by the *American Educator*, a journal of the American Federation of Teachers. This journal publishes some of the best syntheses of good instructional practice, including, among others, high-quality reading instruction especially for children from poverty backgrounds (Torgeson, 2004) and teaching English language learners (Goldenberg, 2008).

Another good source of research syntheses on good instructional practice is *Educational Leadership*, the journal of the Association for Supervision and Curriculum Development. A recent excellent example of such an article is that by Slavin, Chamberlain, and Daniels (2007) on preventing reading failure and developing reading competence for middle and high school students.

Readers also are encouraged to have conversations with other districts and schools that have made large progress in boosting student performance, asking what they did on the curriculum and instructional fronts. Craft wisdom sometimes is ahead of actual research evidence. If a district with similar students does something on the curriculum and instructional front that produces large gains in student achievement, then that is worth knowing.

3. COLLABORATIVE WORK

Teachers worked at developing these views of effective instruction in very collaborative processes—through professional learning communities—as ways to implement new approaches to reading, mathematics, or any other subject. And these new ways of teaching permeated new teacher induction, ongoing professional development for experienced teachers, staff meetings, and often made it into the district's evaluation systems as well. The new approaches to instructional practice became anchors for several of the districts' teacher development programs. In the process, instructional practice became "public," in that teachers talked together about good instructional practice, worked at it in their own classrooms, had it demonstrated for them by instructional coaches, and made the goal that over time all teachers would deploy instruction according to this new vision.

This creation of a shared sense of good instructional practice, together with new curriculum programs, is how teachers made a big difference in student learning. When educators cite the research that teachers have the largest impact on student achievement, what is underneath the claim is teachers' instructional practice—both what they teach and how they teach it. The best teachers deploy different instructional practices than other teachers; that is why they are more effective. The widely known case of District 2 in New York City (Elmore & Burney, 1999) had this as a central core of the district's efforts: All efforts were orchestrated around a new view of how to teach reading. And the schools and districts we studied that doubled performance developed new understandings of effective teaching as well as a culture that required all teachers to learn these instructional practices and use them with their students. Indeed, part of the Madison story is that teachers demanded more and more specifics about the balanced approach to reading instruction that all teachers were expected to implement, and as those views of reading instructional practice took hold in the primary grades, both upper-elementary and middle school teachers asked for the same development focus for those grade levels as well.

4. SUMMARY

In sum, districts and schools adopted a wide variety of curriculum materials and approaches to instructional practice. Though there are some commonalities across these curriculum and instructional approaches, the examples exhibit more variation than commonality. The prime point is that all districts and schools adopted new curriculum and instructional approaches as part of their educational strategies to dramatically improve student achievement.

We have found no case of a school or district that simply worked harder at the curriculum and instructional program that existed when they engaged in the Strategy 1 analysis of their students' state test data. Consciously or unconsciously, they all decided that the old curriculum program had gotten them to their existing performance level, which was not good enough, and that something different, something more powerful and more rigorous, was needed to help them attain their new ambitious goals. Districts and schools also created a point of view about instructional practice that was linked to the new curriculum and that together with that curriculum would boost student learning.

In short, during Strategy 3, schools throw out their old curriculum programs and books and replace them with new curriculum programs, and simultaneously over time collaboratively develop more effective ways to teach that curriculum that all teachers are supposed to learn and implement in their classrooms. They change the curriculum and instructional program and make it systemic across all classrooms and often across all schools in the district. They view this consistency and systemic approach as the professional approach—rather than have each teacher selecting his or her own textbook and teaching according to his or her own personal preferences. The culture for sustaining this perspective was particularly strong in Montgomery County, where the district's own teachers developed most of these instructional approaches, with the assumption that within each school, all teachers were expected to use both the new materials and their collaborative approach to instructional practice.

Going somewhat beyond the data in our cases, I suggest that all schools and districts review the vision of accomplished teaching that is embodied in the 24 standards of the National Board for Professional Teaching Standards. These documents represent a consensus of what many of the top teachers, politicians, and educational and business leaders in this country consider high-quality instruction. Districts could use these standards to "drive" quality instructional practice throughout all schools and classrooms, including developing and placing in lead positions National Board Certified Teachers, that is, individuals who have shown that their instructional practice meets the high and rigorous standards for Board Certification. Though some have interpreted the research on the effectiveness of National Board Certified teachers as somewhat mixed, the most statistically sophisticated studies show that National Board Certified teachers are effective teachers who produce some of the largest student learning gains; Goldhaber, Perry, and Anthony (2004) and Goldhaber and Anthony (2005) show that those who seek National Board Certification are among the best teachers, and that among that group of good teachers, those who become certified produce more learning gains than those who do not get certified.

Chicago, for example, has adopted National Board Certification as an indicator of high-quality teaching (Kimball, 2008). If the district followed through on that policy and infused its major teacher development programs—induction, mentoring, professional development, evaluation, and even compensation—with the vision of effective instruction embodied in the board's standards, it not only would be sending a powerful signal of what, as a district, it believes represents good instructional practice but also would be setting a clear direction toward which each teacher could move in developing their individual instructional repertoire.

NOTES

1. Please see http://ies.ed.gov/ncee/wwc/reports/beginning_reading/open_court for more information.

Benchmark and Formative Assessments and Data-Based Decision Making

It may surprise some readers to learn that Strategy 4 includes adopting and using more testing, even beyond what is required by the state or NCLB (No Child Left Behind). Contrary to the widespread complaints in many education circles that there is too much testing in America's schools, the places that double performance actually add additional layers of testing—benchmark as well as formative assessments. These are not tests per se, but information on student performance that helps teachers hone in on and enhance instructional practice. Indeed, the teachers in the schools that have doubled performance have learned at least two things: (1) To be a continuous improvement system, system performance—student knowledge and achievement—needs to be measured often and used to improve practice, and (2) More small-grained measurements of performance, including formative assessments, can help them make practice more targeted and thus more effective and efficient.

Section 1 provides some general definitions of benchmark and formative assessments and describes some of the most popular systems that were used. Section 2 is a longer description of how formative assessments became one of the key elements of the improvements in Montgomery County

Public Schools. Section 3 makes some comments about value-added measures of student performance.

1. OVERVIEW OF BENCHMARK AND FORMATIVE ASSESSMENTS

Although state tests provide school faculties with a macromap of where the school has been effective in teaching students and areas where it needs to improve, state tests provide feedback on student performance at the *end of the school year,* and the feedback is in summary form that covers what was to be learned over the previous academic year. Such data are only grossly indicative of how to improve performance. Benchmark and formative assessments are student measures given at various times *during the school year* and are used to help teachers alter and enhance practice as the year progresses. Although these two terms—benchmark and formative—are often used as synonyms, they are technically different.

Benchmark Assessments

Benchmark assessments tend to be given periodically, usually quarterly, or about every nine weeks of instruction. They provide "summative" data on student learning, but only for the content taught during the previous nine weeks of instruction. Thus, summed over the course of the year, they provide more detail on student performance than just the annual state tests and, as importantly, provide this information during the school year. Thus, if student performance was lagging, re-teaching could occur to ensure that the subsequent units of instruction, which often require use of the knowledge taught in the previous quarter, would indeed be provided only when the previous content had been learned.

Formative Assessments

Formative assessments generally are more diagnostic in nature and are given at periods *within a nine-week instructional period.* Most often, formative assessments are given before a curriculum unit is taught, thus providing teachers with data on what students know about the content in the unit beforehand; this enables teachers to craft an instructional approach directly tailored to the knowledge of their students.

Formative assessments provide the information a teacher needs to create a micromap for how to teach specific curriculum units. Though analyses of the state tests provide a good beginning for schools to redesign their overall educational program, and benchmark assessments give feedback on each quarter of instruction, teachers also need the additional, more microlevel, formative assessment and other screening data to help them design details and daily lesson plans for each specific curriculum unit in order to become more effective in getting all students to learn the main objectives in each curriculum unit to proficiency.

When teachers have the detailed data from formative assessments, they are able to design instructional activities that are more precisely matched to the exact learning status of the students in their own classrooms and schools. In this way, their instruction can be, to use a term from the business community, much more efficient because they know the goals and objectives they want students to learn: They know exactly what their students do and do not know with respect to those goals and objectives, and thus they can design instructional activities specifically to help the students in their classrooms learn the goals and objectives for the particular curriculum unit.

Many times, teachers, principals, and other education leaders use the term formative assessments to refer to what has been defined above as benchmark assessments, or they use the term benchmark assessments instead of formative assessments. Though the above paragraphs seek to make a clear distinction between benchmark assessments and formative assessments, the issue is not so much using the correct label as it is noting that the high-performance districts and schools, which serve as the basis for the points made in this book, use student achievement data that goes far beyond that available in state tests only. These schools and districts understand that state tests are summative instruments that provide a macropicture of student performance at the end of the school year but are not detailed enough to inform the microstrategies of instructional practice, and that the latter requires additional measures of student performance provided by a combination of benchmark and formative assessments, which are then used to tailor instructional practice to the precise status of the students being taught.

However, although analysis of the macroissues revealed through state assessment analysis is relatively straightforward once faculties in schools are given access to test data, analysis of the microdata from the benchmark and formative assessments and the linkages to revised instructional practices are much more difficult. Analyses of state tests reveal topics that are not taught in the curriculum, such as writing, or expectations that are not met, such as problem solving in mathematics. And these are quite straightforward to remedy—teach more writing and embed more authentic problem solving in the math curriculum.

Benchmark assessments provide feedback at the end of a quarter indicating whether student achievement is sufficiently high to proceed teaching the next set of curriculum units; if student performance is lagging, however, the teacher faces the dilemma of how much time to spend on reteaching versus time needed to cover all the content in the scope and sequence for the course being taught. Nevertheless, benchmark assessment data provide more periodic feedback on student performance that can then be used by teachers as they proceed to provide instruction for subsequent content.

Formative assessment results are even more difficult to translate into instructional practices. When a teacher has the "running record" for his or her 25 elementary students, it is not straightforward to design instructional strategies—whole class, subgroups, or individual approaches—that address the learning profile of each student; creating instructional practice that is tailored to the formative assessments from a classroom of students takes an expertise that most teachers do not have. This means that professional development resources must be used to help teachers design instructional strategies based on the results of formative assessments. See Boudett, City, and Murnane (2007) and the Wireless Generation (www.wirelessgeneration.com) for examples of how to interpret formative assessment data and translate it into concrete and student-specific appropriate instructional strategies.

NWEA MAP Assessments

One commercially available benchmark assessment system, called Measures of Academic Performance (MAP) used by many of the schools and districts that have doubled performance is available from the North West Evaluation Association (www.nwea.org) in Portland, Oregon. This is one of the most popular benchmark assessment systems used across the country, even though many districts actually call these data formative assessments. These assessments are taken by students on a computer, using an Internet-based online system, for a fee of about $7 per student for administration three times a year in only reading and mathematics; because they are online, teachers receive the results the next day and can immediately use them in their weekly instructional planning. The data report not only provides information on student results but also "norms" those results to the school, the district, the state, and the nation. Some districts in North Dakota have used three years of NWEA data for high school students to "predict" scores on college entrance examinations such as the ACT. Thus, NWEA assessment data might have more utility than just as benchmark assessments.

MAP assessments are generally given three times a year, after each quarter of instruction, so they are also more in the benchmark than formative assessment category. Kennewick used the MAP system from the NWEA, nearly all districts surrounding Madison, Wisconsin, use the MAP benchmark assessments during the school year, as do more than 50% of all districts in North Dakota. We know that the bulk of districts, including the largest districts in Wyoming, have also adopted the NWEA-MAP benchmark assessment system.

Early Literacy Formative Assessments

Madison, Wisconsin, taught all teachers to take the running records that are normally part of the Reading Recovery tutoring program and instead use them as the basis for the formative assessment analysis in that district. Many Reading First schools, and some of the schools we have studied, use the Dynamic Indicators of Basic Early Literacy Skills (DIBELS) formative assessments (http://dibels.uoregon.edu). The Wireless Generation Web site has created a formative assessment quite similar to DIBELS that can be used with a handheld, Palm Pilot-like, electronic device. The company also offers a Web service that provides information on how to turn the results into specific instructional strategies; the Web service also provides professional development for teachers, including video clips of how to teach certain reading skills. The cost is about $15 per student per year, plus about $200 per teacher for the device, and somewhat more for training, though the company usually uses a trainer-of-trainers approach. Musti-Rao and Cartledge (2007) identify a number of additional reading-assessment batteries, and Jordan (2007) identifies a screening instrument that assesses number-sense knowledge in elementary children, which is a basic concept for understanding arithmetic.

2. BENCHMARK AND FORMATIVE ASSESSMENTS IN MONTGOMERY COUNTY, MARYLAND

Montgomery County, Maryland, has implemented one of the most comprehensive approaches to using benchmark and formative assessments as a core part of the district's strategies to improve student performance. First, the district set the goal of educating 100% of students to or above the state's proficiency bar—regardless of family background, minority status, home language, or achievement level at the time of initial enrollment in the district.

Back in 2000, when the reform strategies were launched, the district decided initially to focus on the early years, to ensure that the growing numbers of students from lower-income, minority, and ELL backgrounds started school ready to learn. It put a full-day kindergarten program into all schools with high concentrations of children from lower-income backgrounds, then reduced class sizes to 15 for Grades K–2 in those schools, and also launched preschool programs.

Then the district began its approach to improving instructional practice through teacher-developed benchmark and formative assessments and collegial work to use the results to strengthen classroom instruction. Using teachers, the district developed common benchmark assessments that were to be used for all kindergarten children and followed that with a structured, research-based curriculum that was to be used in all full-day kindergarten classrooms. This initiative, focused initially on kindergarten, actually launched a full-scale districtwide curriculum, benchmark, and formative assessment initiative that ultimately covered all grade levels and most content areas. The notion was that school-based teacher teams would use the collaboratively developed benchmark assessment information to craft formative assessments, lesson plans, and curriculum units in ways specifically tailored to the needs of their own students.

To ensure that these collaborative efforts at using benchmark assessment data within schools worked, the district provided extensive professional development in *data-based decision making* and analysis. Professional development focused on analyzing the data school by school as well as classroom by classroom. Teachers were taught how to analyze the data themselves and as members of grade-level (in elementary schools) or content-area (in secondary schools) teams. Teachers would collect the formative and benchmark data and enter it into a district spreadsheet. That system would then identify each child's performance level, which, in turn, would allow the teachers to plan for mixtures of whole-class and group instruction tailored to the specific needs of the children in their grade and classroom. By setting outcome exit standards for all kindergarten students, standards that would allow them to do well in first grade, the training in data analysis was focused on helping (grade-level) teacher teams analyze the benchmark assessment data to create classroom strategies designed to enable all students, regardless of their entering performance status, to meet the kindergarten exit proficiency standards by the end of the school year. In other words, student benchmark assessment data analyses were directed toward common grade-level outcome goals, regardless of the entry-status level of performance.

A similar process of developing formative assessments leading to instructional strategies was then created for all core content areas and all grade levels.

Professional development then addressed a variety of instructional strategies:

- How to pace teaching the curriculum
- Prerequisite skills children needed in order to learn how to read
- How to use benchmark and formative assessment data to craft curriculum units that matched student needs, guided by professional knowledge of how students learned to read
- How and when to provide whole-group instruction or to create small groups
- What to teach in the small groups
- What to do if children were not understanding what was being taught
- Next steps for struggling students

Many of the strategies and techniques were taken from research, drawing from the multiple partnerships the district created with local universities. In sum, the professional development was comprehensive, focused on linking data on student performance (formative, benchmark, and the state summative data) to grouping and instructional strategies, and geared to teachers' producing common high outcomes for all kindergarten students, regardless of background.

Initially there was pushback from teachers for these collaborative approaches to using a common curriculum, collaborative data analysis, pacing charts, monitoring of implementation, and ensuring that no child fell behind. But over time, according to both teachers and administrators interviewed, the bulk of teachers began to see the power of the system and came to accept the system, while simultaneously seeing their students' performance rise.

One highly improving elementary school reflects well on how the collaborative approach to data-based decision making around formative assessments works in this district. This PreK–5 school enrolls about 500 students, 67% of whom are Title I eligible, with most representing minority and ELL backgrounds. Reflecting the district, the school's goal is to educate *all* (emphasis noted by school staff interviewed) students to the grade-level proficiency standards in Maryland, regardless of poverty or ELL status or entry performance level. And the school has had considerable success. Between 90 and 95% of all the students score at or above proficiency on the state standards, as do all major subgroups—Title I eligible students, ELL students, and Hispanic students. The school has delivered on its goal. According to teachers, the core reason for the good results is consistency of curriculum and instruction, which is held together by a collaborative professional school culture that evolves from the collaborative teams the school has created.

Grade-level teams, organized into Professional Learning Communities (PLCs), are the "engines" of the school. These teams set goals together; review student data; talk about individual students; analyze formative, benchmark, and summative assessments; create content "maps" from which they develop curriculum units that are used by all grade-level teachers and that combine over the course of the year to cover the Maryland curriculum standards for their grade; and work together to increase curriculum and instructional expertise for all the teachers in their grade-level team. The teams create common curriculum units that each teacher in the team actually teaches.

Further, the teachers have made an additional advance in curriculum and assessment consistency by using *common end-of-curriculum-unit assessments* for each curriculum unit they have collaboratively created. These student performance results allow the grade-level teams to review the performance of all students in a grade to the standard of the common assessments; this allows the teams to identify what worked and what did not, to add ideas to the units from the teachers who were particularly effective, and to note and provide assistance to colleagues whose students did not do that well.

Over the years, teachers at all grade levels in this school created the school's own formative assessments; they used the district benchmark assessments as a foundation, but the formative assessments were more micro. All assessments created by the school, however, are aligned with the Maryland Learning Outcomes. As a result, all the teachers in each grade-level team work with a set of common formative assessments, common curriculum-unit assessments, and common benchmark quarterly assessments, all of which are linked to the state's summative assessments. By developing their own formative assessments over the years, the teachers have been better able to understand what the Maryland outcome assessments actually mean and require from students, and what teachers need to do to produce students who perform successfully on those assessments.

A district-provided "staff-development teacher" is provided to all elementary schools in the district, and helps each grade-level team to align their battery of assessments not only to the state tests but also across each grade level. This further improved the consistency of instruction both across classes within grades and across grades within the school; indeed, all teachers at each grade level teach the same units at the same time and then use common-unit assessments to determine how well students learned. Since the school has been moving from assessment data to instructional strategies in a collaborative manner for several years, it has developed considerable expertise in how to assess a battery of 80 formative assessments for all the students in a grade and translate that into instructional strategies that work.

As a result, teachers in this school do not "do their own thing in the classroom." They use and implement the commonly developed curriculum units and end-of-unit common assessments. They view teaching as a collaborative effort and teachers within a grade level as interdependent, including the preschool and kindergarten teachers. Moreover, individual grade-level teachers view all students at a grade level as "their own" students. Grade-level teams review performance data from all students in the grade and then take various actions, for instance, grouping students across sections within a grade for certain topics or having certain teachers who are especially good with some student problems instruct those students with those problems. The point is that the team works collaboratively, varying student grouping and teacher assignment to get all the students at that grade level up to grade-level proficiency.

The prime impact of the school, according to teachers and administrators interviewed, is the high-quality, common-core instructional program in all key curriculum areas at each grade level, which is articulated across grades and aligned with Maryland's content standards. The foundations for this consistent instructional approach are the district's benchmark assessments, the school's formative assessments, and common end-of-curriculum-unit assessments, all of which are tied to the district's and state's content standards and proficiency standards, and used by teacher teams to craft and refine commonly used curriculum units over the course of the full school year.

3. A COMMENT ON VALUE-ADDED MEASURES

Data-based decision making generally refers to using a combination of summative, benchmark, and formative assessments of student performance, as well as common end-of-curriculum-unit tests, to assess the impact of instructional practice and to improve it over time. The goal is to craft instructional practice tightly around detailed teacher knowledge about the achievement and learning status of their specific students.

A second aspect of data-based decision making, however, concerns teacher performance and effectiveness. The goal of this focus of decision making is to determine the degree to which there is variation across teachers in producing student achievement, factors behind that variation in effectiveness, and how that knowledge can be used to improve and make teacher performance more consistent and more impactful across the district over time. The state test data, the benchmark data, and the common end-of-curriculum-unit data could be used to construct simple trend analysis for each classroom as an approach to indicate the effectiveness of each individual teacher.

But another type of increasingly popular data-based decision making on school and classroom effectiveness is generally based on various forms of value-added analyses. To conduct such value-added analyses, the district needs a database that links the achievement scores of every student to the teacher who taught that subject to the student. Though conceptually simple, developing a database that accurately matches students to teachers is not straightforward; for example, one would need to identify which teacher taught each student reading in an elementary school that regrouped students across grades for reading instruction. Nevertheless, several districts and states have moved forward and have developed such a database.

The results can show which teachers "add more value," that is, produce more learning to student achievement as compared to others. Such analyses of teacher effectiveness can generally indicate the top 10 to 20% of teachers and the bottom 10 to 20% of teachers in terms of their effectiveness, but the analysis has difficulty at this point reliably distinguishing teacher effectiveness for those individuals in the middle 60% of the performance range. The Value Added Research Center (VARC) at the University of Wisconsin–Madison is working with many districts on these issues, and its Web site has many readable documents on the advantages and shortcomings of this analytic procedure (http://varc.wceruw.org).

Some districts and schools have studied the instructional practice of the top-performing teachers and have found that they teach reading or mathematics differently; they have then turned those instructional practices into professional development for other teachers. The teacher recruitment organization Teach For America also conducted this analysis and developed its Teaching as Leadership standards on the basis of the resulting analysis (www.teachforamerica.org). Other places have used the results from value-added analysis at the classroom level to indicate which teachers need intensive professional development. Indeed, research has shown that students with teachers at the bottom of the range of value-added actually lose relative achievement standing over the course of a year; such teachers need significant extra help and if their practice does not improve, counseling to some nonteaching position.

When systems develop such a student-linked-to-teacher and even linked-to-school database, it also can be used to evaluate the impact of various educational interventions at either the school or teacher level. The database and value-added analysis can answer such questions as: Did reading program X work? Did professional development program Y work? And so forth.

Thus, districts and schools seeking to dramatically improve student performance should move forward to create such student-teacher-school-linked database systems. Results from appropriate value-added analyses using such data systems can add substantial additional information to good performance management of the overall education system, which is always asking the question about the effectiveness of any intervention.

4. SUMMARY

It is an irony in this age of criticism about too much testing that the schools and districts doubling performance actually expanded testing. To be sure, these high-performance educational organizations agreed that mere testing did not make students learn more. However, they stated very strongly that although state tests provided them with an overall, summary picture of student performance in the school—identifying areas of high, average, and low performance—benchmark and formative assessments were also needed during the school year to provide more nuanced micromaps for how they needed to teach specific curriculum units and to boost performance that the macrotests measured. And one of the most recent aspects of this comprehensive approach to data-based decision making is the use of common end-of-curriculum-unit tests; such instruments not only provide teachers and the overall system with a measure of how students achieved but also use reliable data to compare teacher impact across classrooms, which can lead to both intervention strategies as well as studying the top performers to determine what they did to produce those high levels of student achievement gains.

In short, benchmark and formative assessments are a new but rapidly evolving educational tool (see Boudett & Steele, 2007; Boudett et al., 2007; Informative Assessment, 2007/2008). And there are many sources and types of these assessments. New York City uses benchmark assessments (Goertz & Levin, 2008); Long Beach created its own formative assessments (Koppich, 2008), as did Madison (Odden & Archibald, 2009). Montgomery County developed its own benchmark and formative assessments. And several schools and districts use commercially available benchmark and formative assessments.

Two 2008 reports commissioned by the New Schools Venture Fund (Datnow, Park, & Kennedy, 2008; Datnow, Park, & Wohlstetter, 2008) provide more detail on how several districts and both elementary and secondary schools have used data to improve instruction and in the process boosted student achievement.

A Comment on Resources. It should be clear that the first four strategies require very modest resources. As noted, purchasing access to formative assessments costs approximately $25 to $35 per student, hardly a big dent in any district budget and increasingly an expenditure that districts and schools doubling performance are managing to squeeze into their budgets. Though analyzing state test scores, setting high goals and expectations, and reviewing and then adopting new curriculum and instruction programs takes some time, the activities themselves require at most a small amount of money. Buying new textbooks and instructional materials takes money, but all districts already have funds for such expenditures, so in the medium term, those expenditures can be absorbed into ongoing regular budgets. The next strategies, however, require a more significant level of resources to implement.

Provide Ongoing, Intensive Professional Development

At this point it will not be a surprise to read that the next strategy in the doubling student performance process is providing widespread, systemic, intensive, and ongoing professional development. This was a uniform finding from all schools and districts, and it makes good sense. Often, the initial analysis of state testing data entails some professional development, as not all teachers and principals are skilled in analyzing the full meaning and all the implications of state test data. Further, the adoption of new curriculum programs requires additional professional development to help all teachers acquire the expertise to teach the new curricular materials well; moreover, most of the professional development linked to the new textbooks and other curriculum materials was provided by district staff or other consultants, not the textbook companies. In addition, extensive and ongoing professional development is needed as the schools and districts work to develop the system's new approach to good instruction; such professional development around new instructional practices continues for several years and had not stopped in any of the places that doubled performance. Finally, considerable professional development is needed for teachers to develop the expertise to take the information from the many benchmark and especially formative assessments and based on that data design instructional strategies that meet the needs of the students in each of their classrooms.

This chapter has three sections. The first section summarizes the key features that make professional development programs work and the resource needs of those features. Section 2 describes the kind of general approach to professional development that has emerged in most of the schools and districts studied and shows how it is different from the popular approach of having each teacher create his or her own professional development plan.

1. THE FEATURES OF EFFECTIVE PROFESSIONAL DEVELOPMENT[1]

Effective professional development is defined as professional development that produces change in teachers' classroom-based instructional practice, which can be linked to improvements in student learning. The emerging consensus on what characterizes "high-quality" or "effective" professional development draws on a series of empirical research studies that link program strategies to changes in teachers' instructional practice and subsequent increases in student achievement. These studies include, among others, (1) the long-term efforts of Bruce Joyce (Joyce & Calhoun, 1996; Joyce & Showers, 2002), (2) research on the change process (Fullan, 2001), (3) a longitudinal analysis of efforts to improve mathematics in California (Cohen & Hill, 2001), (4) Elmore's study of District 2 in New York City (Elmore & Burney, 1999), (5) the Consortium for Policy Research in Education's longitudinal study of sustained professional development provided by the Merck Institute for Science Education (Supovitz & Turner, 2000), (6) studies of comprehensive professional development to improve science teaching and learning (Loucks-Horsley, Love, Stiles, Mundry, & Hewson, 2003), and (7) an evaluation of the federal Eisenhower mathematics and science professional development program (Garet, Birman, Porter, Desimone, & Herman, 1999; Porter, Garet, Desimone, & Birman, 2003).

In summarizing the key features of effective professional development, analysts (e.g., Elmore, 2002; Joyce & Showers, 2002; Odden & Archibald, 2009; Odden, Archibald, Fermanich, & Gallagher, 2002) have identified six structural features of such programs:

1. The **form** of the activity—that is, whether the activity is organized as a study group, teacher network, workshop, mentoring collaborative, committee, or curriculum development group. The above research suggests that effective professional development should be school-based, job-embedded, ongoing, and focused on the curriculum taught rather than just a one-day workshop.

2. The **duration** of the activity, including the total number of contact hours that participants are expected to spend in the activity, as well as the span of time over which the activity takes place. The above research has shown the importance of continuous, ongoing, long-term professional development that totals many hours annually, at least 100 hours and closer to 200 hours.

3. The degree to which the activity emphasizes the **collective participation** of teachers from the same school, department, or grade level. The above research suggests that effective professional development should be organized around groups of teachers from a school that over time would include everyone in the school— that is, the *entire faculty.*

4. The degree to which the activity has a **content focus**—that is, the degree to which the activity is focused on improving and deepening teachers' content knowledge as well as how students learn that content. The above research concludes that effective professional development focuses on the content of the curriculum the teachers will teach, including the common student miscues or problems students typically have learning that content, and on effective instructional strategies for that content.

5. The extent to which the activity offers opportunities for **active learning**, such as opportunities for teachers to become engaged in the meaningful analysis of teaching and learning; for example, by scoring student work, assessing formative assessment data and designing instructional practice based on that data, or developing and refining a standards-based curriculum unit. The above research has shown that professional development is most effective when it includes opportunities for teachers to work directly on incorporating the new techniques into their instructional practice with the help of instructional coaches.

6. The degree to which the activity promotes **coherence** in teachers' professional development by aligning professional development to other key parts of the education system such as student content and performance standards, teacher evaluation, school and district goals, and the development of a professional community.

Form, duration, and active learning together imply that effective professional development includes some initial learning in training sessions (such as a two-week, 10-day, summer training institute) as well as considerable longer-term work in which teachers work collaboratively at their school on curriculum and instructional issues and incorporate the new methodologies into their actual classroom practice.

Active learning implies some degree of coaching during regular school hours to help the teacher incorporate new strategies into his or her normal instructional practices; in Montgomery County, for example, this would include the time when all teachers worked on creating or refining curriculum units incorporating the results of formative assessments, taught that curriculum unit—oftentimes with assistance from the instructional coach—and when they debriefed the unit as a teacher team.

It should be clear that the longer the duration, and the more coaching, the more time is required of teachers as well as professional development trainers and coaches.

Content focus means that effective professional development focuses largely on subject matter knowledge, what is known about how students learn that subject, and the content in the actual curriculum used in the school. In the context of a specific school and specific curriculum and textbook, the professional development would focus on both the content of each curriculum unit and the content-specific pedagogy, as well as on the general pedagogy needed to teach that unit effectively.

Collective participation implies that the best professional development includes groups of, and at some point *all* teachers in a school or district, who then work together to implement the new instructional strategies and in the process build a professional school community. This implies that professional development is not a voluntary but a professional activity in which all teachers in the school are expected to engage.

Coherence suggests that the professional development is more effective when the signals from the policy environment (federal, state, district, and school) reinforce rather than contradict one another or send multiple, confusing messages. Coherence also implies that professional development opportunities should be provided as part of implementing new curriculum programs in addition to implementing the district's or school's vision of effective instructional approaches.

Note that there is little support in this research for the development of individually oriented professional development plans; the research implies a much more systemic approach that involves all teachers (at a grade level in elementary school or content area in secondary schools) in the school working together on translating formative assessment data into instructional strategies, learning more deeply the content to be taught, working together to refine curriculum units that are linked to the curriculum standards and the textbook used, and collectively debriefing on how each unit went (see also Hirsh & Killion, 2009). To be sure, some professional development could be tailored, for example, to the needs of brand-new teachers, to more experienced novices in their third to fifth year of teaching, and to more senior teachers. But the finding about coherence and collective participation implies that professional development is a collegial activity and not an individualistic activity. Indeed, when a district adopts a new curriculum program, all teachers would need at least some professional development. Moreover, as districts and schools create their view of effective instructional practice over time, all teachers need to be engaged in activities to learn these instructional strategies.

In the Montgomery County context, moreover, one can see both the systemic nature of professional development and how the needs of new and experienced teachers can be handled simultaneously. As teachers work in grade-level teams, for example, assume the team consists of a new teacher, two teachers with three to six years of experience, and a more senior teacher, all of whom are working with the school's instructional coach. In this context, the brand new teacher is not working alone and for all curriculum units has access to the units and their lesson plans that the team has produced in the past. The new teacher participates in all planning and collaborative tasks, which would probably be chaired by the senior teacher functioning as the grade-level team coordinator, and all four teachers would draw on the expertise of the instructional coach, called a "professional development teacher," in that district. In this kind of an arrangement for the ongoing collaborative work of teachers, it would be hard to imagine how each teacher would create his or her "own" professional development plan, because each teacher's professional development would in fact be embedded in these multiple professional collaborative interactions—translating formative data into instructional practices, honing curriculum units and lesson plans, teaching common curriculum units, and then collaboratively debriefing.

Resource Requirements of Effective Professional Development[2]

It should be noted that each of these six structural features has resource requirements. Form, duration, collective participation, and active learning require various amounts of both teacher and trainer/coach/mentor time during the regular school day and year and, depending on the specific strategies, outside of the regular day and year as well. This time costs money. Further, all professional development strategies require some amount of administration, materials and supplies, and miscellaneous financial support for travel and fees.

Pupil-Free Days

To be more concrete, there are three primary resources needed to mount the type of professional development programs found in the schools and districts that have doubled performance. The first is pupil-free teacher days, during which time teachers receive training. Pupil-free days can be accomplished in two ways. One way is by hiring substitute teachers and providing professional development during the regular school year; unless the student year is extended, though, this strategy reduces time for teachers to instruct students and was therefore the least-followed strategy in the schools and districts studied. The other way to provide pupil-free days is by extending the school year for teachers and providing the training part of professional development during the summer before the school year starts (a strategy that does not require extending the school year for students), or during days spaced throughout the year when students are not present (which in order not to reduce instructional time for students would mean the student academic year also would need to be extended). To provide the appropriate remuneration, teachers are paid either a daily stipend for these days or the teacher contract year is extended at the average daily rate. The cost for either is about the same. Many of the schools and districts studied provided approximately ten days of pupil-free time for teacher professional development and, again, most often these days were used in the summer for training.

Training Funds

A second cost is funds for trainers. Whether the trainers are external consultants, technical assistance providers, part of comprehensive school designs, or central-office professional development staff, funds are needed to cover the training costs. In a few cases, districts were able to access support staff from regional education offices but most often even these individuals charged fees for services provided, especially if they were long-term services. An estimate of training costs is $100 per pupil.

Instructional Coaches

A third cost is for instructional facilitators, or instructional coaches. These are individuals who work in schools, often on a full-time basis, and provide the in-classroom coaching assistance that is key to making professional work lead to change in instructional practice that produces student learning gains. The creation of instructional coach, lead teacher, professional development teacher, mentor, and head-teacher positions, all labels for essentially the same role, distinguishes the professional development initiatives from most of those in the past and appears to be a "secular" trend around the country. An estimate of the need for instructional coaches is one full-time equivalent (FTE) coach position for every 200 students; in a 400-student elementary school, this would produce 2 FTE coach positions, which could be filled by a full-time reading coach, a half-time math coach, and a half-time science coach, so all coaching positions would not need to be full time (Odden & Picus, 2008).

Odden and Archibald (2009) discuss how schools and districts reallocated resources to fund some of these professional development costs. The above summary of resources is simply to describe here the elements that were needed to deploy the kinds of intensive and ongoing professional development found in many of the schools and districts that have dramatically improved student achievement.

Collaborative Time During the Regular School Day

Another requirement for professional development, which tends to be resourced "separately" from a professional development budget, is some time during the regular school day for collaboration among teachers and the instructional coaches on the instructional program. Wei, Andree, and Darling-Hammond (2009) note that high-achieving countries build time for professional learning into most teachers' workday. This resource allows for the "job embedded" aspect of ongoing professional development. This is the time when teacher teams analyze formative assessments, create instructional units, or debrief on how the units went. This time is usually available if the school has staff for elective classes such as art, music, and physical education, because when students are in elective classes their regular content teachers are not teaching and have time (if all grade-level teachers or content teachers have their planning and prep period at the same time) to collaborate on curriculum and instruction; if elective teachers are not provided, then schools usually extend the teacher work day to provide time for teacher collaborative work.

As just stated, some of the most collaborative professional development occurs when groups of teachers meet, usually with the instructional coaches, to discuss the results of the formative assessments and create new teaching strategies and instructional units specifically tailored to the needs of the students as revealed in the formative assessment data.[3] This is complex work. Often, the instructional coach is able to identify professional development topics for teachers, based on the struggles teachers might have in moving from the assessment data to finely honed instructional units. So the products of these sessions are both professional development for teachers and more finely targeted curriculum units and instructional strategies for students. Smith, Wilson, and Corbett (2009) argue in one of their most recent articles that trained facilitators or instructional coaches are one of the key conditions that help to make teacher collaborative work on instructional practice effective. These are the kinds of ongoing teacher collaborative work that resulted in the creation of professional learning communities in nearly all of the schools and districts that have doubled student performance.

In this process, professional development mentoring is provided to new and experienced teachers and can be extraordinarily helpful in guiding new teachers successfully into the teaching profession, while at the same time helping experienced teachers broaden their instructional expertise. Shulman and Sato (2006) provide guidance for how to structure effective mentoring programs.

2. EXAMPLES OF PROFESSIONAL DEVELOPMENT PROGRAMS

The above findings from research are fully aligned with the professional development strategies deployed by the schools and districts that doubled performance. However, it is important to describe the ways in which many of the ongoing professional development strategies in the doubling-performance schools operated. See Table 5.1 for the characteristics of more commonly occurring types of professional development versus the specific characteristics of professional development in the schools that doubled performance.

Addressing the latter, many districts offer a central menu of professional development offerings. These could cover multiple topics, from training in leadership skills to cooperative learning to something focused on a content area. The operation of such programs is that teachers would

Table 5.1 Popular Versus Targeted Professional Development Approaches

Popular Professional Development Approaches	Professional Development Strategies in Schools That Doubled Performance
• Districts offer a menu of professional development offerings covering multiple topics. • Teachers decide on their own which offerings to take. • Programs are offered in locations outside the school. • Takes the position that most district-provided professional development does not meet the needs of teachers. • Often the principal or central office has to "sign off" on each teacher's program.	• Focused, systemic, holistic, organic, aligned, collegial, and ongoing practice. • Reflective of the new principles for professional development established by the National Staff Development Council (NSDC). • Professional learning in team-based settings involving all teachers in the school. • Restructuring the school day to provide common collaboration time. • Linking learning directly to the school's curriculum. • Focusing on improved teaching practice and increased student learning.

decide on their own, largely individualistically, which offering to take, and most of which would be offered in locations outside the school. This kind of professional development approach was not found in the districts and schools doubling performance or certainly was not the dominant form of professional development.

Another popular professional development approach takes the position that most district-provided professional development does not meet the needs of teachers. Thus, this second approach puts the teacher in charge of identifying his or her professional development needs. In this context, each teacher creates his or her own professional development plan; often the plan is required to be linked to a teaching standard, a school goal, and a district goal. The objective of these linkage requirements is to connect the teacher's professional development actions to something important to the district. Often the principal, and sometimes even the central office, has to sign off or approve each teacher's professional development program. Sometimes a team, usually composed of some members outside of the teacher's school, approves the program and then certifies at the end of the year whether the teacher has implemented the plan. This professional development approach is required for teachers to earn the professional license in Wisconsin, for example, and is part of the Denver professional compensation program (Heneman & Kimball, 2008). This kind of "teacher atomistic" professional development approach was also not found in the districts and schools doubling performance.

The kinds of professional development programs and approaches found in the schools and districts doubling performance were more focused, more systemic, more holistic, more organic, more aligned, and more collegial. The kinds of professional development found in the districts and schools doubling performance reflect the set of new principles for effective professional development by leaders of the National Staff Development Council (NSDC), Stephanie Hirsh and Joellen Killion (2007, 2009). The main point of the new approaches is that the focus is on professional learning—this happens in team-based settings that involve all teachers in the school, using time provided by the restructuring of the school day to provide common collaboration time, and linking the learning directly to the school's curriculum with the focus on improved teaching practice and increased student learning, with high standards for both.

For example, when the schools or districts adopted a new textbook or curriculum program, professional development on teaching that textbook was often provided for all teachers during pupil-free days both during the summer before the school year began and during some days over the course of the school year—and *all* teachers attended the training. This up-front training would start the professional development in this particular content area and for the textbook selected.

As another example, since all districts and schools eventually created a view of instructional practice that was considered effective in that context, all teachers needed professional development for this instructional approach. Before the full vision of this instructional approach was articulated, many teachers were part of the professional development experiences that over time led to a district/systemic conceptualization of effective instructional practices, which the system then wanted all teachers to learn and use. Subsequent summer professional development sessions, then, focused intensively on the district's effective instructional vision, and the system had goals to have all teachers engaged in such professional development experiences.

As a third example, recall the description of the work in Montgomery County, and read the following as "in addition" to the previous three examples. The first step involved curriculum mapping to produce a grade-by-grade curriculum scope and sequence that was matched to and aligned with the state's curriculum standards. Groups of grade-level or content teachers worked collaboratively to produce this result.

Then, within each school, teams of teachers created formative assessments for shorter curriculum units aligned with the scope and sequence and that "added up" over the course of the year to cover all the material in the scope and sequence. In elementary schools, these formative assessments were developed by all teachers in different grade-level teams (Kindergarten, Grade 1, Grade 2, and so on), and in secondary schools these formative assessments were developed by all teachers in various content areas (mathematics, reading/English language arts, science, world language, for example).

Further, these teacher teams also created common curriculum units with common lesson plans, as well as common end-of-unit assessments that all students would take.

In all these cases, all teachers worked together on common issues; there was virtually no place for "individual" professional development plans; in fact, such plans would have been inappropriate and out of sync with the nature of the teacher collaborative work in these schools.

Further, in the honing of each curriculum unit before it was jointly taught, teachers in the various teams would discuss the overall nature of the curriculum unit, the results of the formative assessments given to their students this year, and the implications for changes in lesson plans or instructional strategies given this year's formative assessment data. Again, an individualistic plan would have been out of line with this collaborative work.

Finally, after teaching the unit and giving the common end-of-unit assessments, the teams then would meet again to debrief on how the unit went, how well the students learned, the performance of each teacher's students, and what was needed to improve the unit the next time around. Again, this would be done collaboratively by all teachers in the team.

These approaches to professional development include all teachers all the time, beginning with the summer institutes; involve all new teachers in all the collaborative meetings throughout the school year; and have new teachers benefit from the past work and existing experience and expertise of all the other teachers and instructional coaches during the work and analysis of the collaborative teams, thus inducting the new person into the professional community. To a significant degree, there is no separate "new teacher induction" program; new teacher induction is embedded into the ongoing collaborative work of teacher teams within each school. This approach to professional development is also more than compatible with summer institutes that focus on both content and pedagogy linked to the specific curriculum materials to be taught but that emphasize the up-front training that is needed. The training would then be implemented through the collaborative teams over the course of the entire next school year.

To be sure, this approach to professional development could be augmented with special sessions, for example, for new teachers on classroom management, for midcareer teachers on translating formative assessment data into instructional practice, for senior teachers on designing curriculum units for advanced problem-solving student goals, and for instructional coaches on how to engage in effective coaching for new, midcareer, and senior teachers. But the major point of the preceding paragraphs is to describe the integrated, ongoing, job-embedded, and collaborative professional development that is characteristic of many of the districts and schools doubling performance and how awkward it would be in those contexts to have a so-called professional development strategy that had each teacher creating his or her own professional development plan.

3. SUMMARY

Professional development was a core, critical, and ongoing practice in the schools and districts that have produced large improvements in student achievement. In many cases, professional development became embedded in the ongoing work of teachers as they worked with their grade-level or content area colleagues in analyzing the implications of formative assessments, developing and refining standards-based curriculum units, and assessing the implications of the student performance results of common end-of-unit assessments that indicated how successfully each unit was and variation of impact across students and teachers.

The resources for these professional development strategies were significant and included time during the regular school day (provided by having elective classes so teachers had planning and preparation periods) for collaborative work on the curriculum and instructional program, additional pupil-free days for training, funds for paying trainers whether provided by central-office staff or external consultants, and instructional coaches in schools. In some cases, schools and districts provided the funds for these resources by reallocating resources, and in other cases they were supported by special grants (such as Reading First) or by funds from an adequacy-oriented school funding reform. And sometimes all the resources were somewhat temporary and the full range of the professional development program could be operated for only one or two years.

But in all cases the bulk of professional development was operated continuously, and the intent was to keep it operating for the long term. The assumption was that student improvement was needed and that the core route to producing those higher levels of achievement was to continuously improve the instructional program, so there was no intent to cut back on the ongoing professional development strategies, particularly the ongoing collaborative work of teachers each week in the school.

Last, it should be noted again that the professional development strategies were ongoing, included all teachers in each school, focused directly on the curriculum that was being taught and the textbook being used, and were not subject to voluntary participation by teachers either picking classes to attend from a central-office set of program offerings or designing their own professional development plans. Professional development was an integral part of the ongoing job of teachers; participation was expected by all teachers as a part of their professional obligations and, in operation, had new, midcareer, and master teachers working in teams continuously to improve professional practice.

NOTES

1. This section draws from Odden and Picus (2008).

2. All these resources are included in the Odden and Picus (2008) school finance adequacy model.

3. Instructional coaches are individuals who work with teachers in many different ways to improve instructional practice. They might be referred to by several different labels, including instructional facilitators, master teachers, mentor teachers, staff development teachers, instructional coaches, and so on.

Using Time Efficiently and Effectively

Strategy 6 concerns the use of what is generally considered a fixed resource—instructional time during the regular school day. Schools and districts doubling student performance used time more effectively and more efficiently.

The chapter has three sections. The first addresses the issue of whether the school days or year should be longer, as that seems to be a popular policy idea that emerges periodically. The second discusses how these schools and districts used time during the traditional school day and year more effectively and efficiently. The third is a short summary of key points.

1. EXTENDING THE SCHOOL YEAR AND DAY

Every other year, it seems, policy makers at federal, state, and local levels make comments that the United States should extend both the school year and the school day as a strategy to improve student learning; the notion is that more time spent in school would lead to more learning. Often, higher levels of student performance in other countries such as Japan, Korea, Singapore, or China, all of which have longer school years and sometimes longer school days as well, are cited as the rationale for these recommendations. But real actions on the suggestion are rare, as they are expensive and there is controversy over whether mere extensions of either the school day or school year would make a difference in student performance (for a recent overview of the arguments, see Cuban, 2008).

First, though many other countries do have longer school days and years than the United States, including those mentioned in the preceding paragraph, those education systems actually use fewer hours of that time for instruction in academic subjects such as reading, mathematics, writing, science, and so on. Average instructional hours in those subjects across the United States during a shorter school year are typically higher than other countries, including many countries in Asia (Organization for Economic Co-operation and Development, 2005). Thus, more time is not the reason students in those countries perform at higher levels than students in the United States.[1]

Those who have studied the international assessments of student performance attribute the differences primarily to differences in curriculum. Hiebert and colleagues (2005), Schmidt (1983), and Stigler and Hiebert (1999) have shown that other countries' curriculum in reading but especially in mathematics and science is both more rigorous and more focused than it is in the United States. They argue the nature of the curriculum and how it is taught are the primary factors in the different achievement levels across countries. The math and science curriculum in too many states and districts in this country is too broad and shallow compared to these other countries. And instructional practice focuses much less on authentic problem solving. Too much instruction is procedural and factual. Too little of instruction in the United States includes real problem solving, and often tends to dumb down the problems so that they are procedural and not authentic.

Thus, these analysts would say that a mere extension of school time in the United States would have little effect on student learning. The same analysts also would argue that focusing the curriculum on covering fewer and core topics in depth, making the curriculum more rigorous, and including authentic problem-solving tasks would be much more powerful in boosting student learning (strategies that most schools and districts doubling performance incorporated into their systems).

As noted in Chapter 7, schools and districts did extend time for struggling students, but the purpose of these actions was to provide additional help to students struggling to learn the core curriculum and to provide that help with different instructional approaches. The remainder of this chapter shows, however, that in addition to having a more rigorous curriculum, the schools and districts doubling student performance did use extant time more effectively.

2. BETTER USES OF TIME

There are several examples of how schools and districts made better use of the time that was provided in the regular school day and regular school year; nearly all of these strategies were "no cost" strategies in the sense that extra money was not needed for these time extensions. None of the schools or districts doubling performance actually extended the school day or year for all students; their time strategies for all students involved using time during the regular school day and year more effectively and, as noted, extending time only for students who were struggling.

Elementary Schools

Elementary schools used such strategies as protecting time for core subjects, extending instructional time for reading and mathematics, maximizing the use of allocated time for instruction, and extending learning time for students struggling to learn to standards.

Protecting Instructional Time for Core Subjects

First, nearly all districts and schools "protected" instructional time for core elementary subjects, particularly mathematics and reading. The time when instruction was being provided for these subjects, especially at the elementary level, was buffeted from interruptions, intercom messaging, trips to the principal's office, and so on. Everyone in the school knew that this time was to be used to provide instruction in reading and mathematics and was to be used for nothing else. This might seem too simple a strategy, but in many of the schools, protection of important instructional time had not been provided in the past, and such protection was easy to implement, once it was decided as a policy by the administration and communicated to teachers.

Extending Time for Some Subjects

Second, most elementary schools set aside a large amount of time for the most important subjects, particularly math and reading. As science begins to be tested under federal and state regulations, it could be expected that science time too will experience similar time policy. For reading in particular, most schools and districts generally set aside 90 minutes a day for various kinds of reading instruction (phonics, word knowledge, comprehension, grammar, writing) but in some cases (Kennewick, Washington, for one), 120 minutes per day were devoted to reading.

Maximize Effective Use of Instructional Time

Third, these gross time allocations were then reinforced by other strategies to maximize the "academic learning time" (ALT) during these formally allocated instructional minutes. ALT is the time that is most correlated to student learning; formally, ALT is the time during which instruction is actually provided and during which students are actually engaged. Even if 90 minutes is allocated for reading, organizational issues of getting the class going and ending the class, or movements among reading groups, for example, could erode those minutes to a smaller number. ALT, then, is the time that actually counts as effective use of the macro-instructional minutes.

One way several schools opted to maximize ALT was to organize students into cross-age groups based on their reading achievement levels; all students were put into classes so that in general students were at the same place in their reading level. In this way, teachers could use the bulk of the 90 minutes for whole-group instruction; they did not have to divide students into different reading groups. Schools that did not use such student grouping generally divided the students into three or more groups at different reading levels. As a result, however, because the teacher needed to spend time separately with each group, students in the other groups did not receive instruction during the time the teacher was with a different group. Though students in the groups not receiving instruction were supposed to be engaged in other reading activities, the fact is that without a teacher, student engagement time was not as intensive as it was when the teacher was present.

One of the schools studied in Kennewick used a combination of both of these strategies during their 120-minute reading block. One hour was spent in whole-group instruction with the classroom teacher, and one hour was spent in small-group instruction, where the small-group instruction was made possible by having almost every staff member in the school teach a reading block. While some grades were having their hour of whole-group instruction, others were having small-group time, and then the school switches, maximizing the number of instructors available for small-group instruction. This allows small groups to be approximately four to nine students for every teacher, where "teacher" can also mean instructional aide, all of whom were trained in the school's *Open Court* reading curriculum. In this way, moreover, students had 60 minutes of instruction in a large group, and then another 60 minutes in a smaller group, and did get a total of 120 minutes of overall reading instruction (though not all 120 minutes would be ALT). As detailed in Odden and Archibald (2009), another part of this strategy was to assign the teachers most skilled in teaching reading to the students struggling most with the reading curriculum, which made instructional time for the struggling students even more effective.

This multiage grouping approach is supported in the broader literature as the most effective way to group students for instruction at least in the early elementary grades (Gutierrez & Slavin, 1992; Mason & Burns, 1996; Mason & Stimson, 1996; Pavan, 1992; Veenman, 1995). Such schools also gave benchmark assessments often, every eight to nine weeks, and regrouped students as a result so that the initial grouping was not set for the year and also did not impact grouping in other subjects—that is, they did not "track" students.

Providing More Time for Struggling Students

Fourth, though the book discusses an additional time extension in more detail in the next chapter, after providing more and more protected minutes of ALT for core subjects, most elementary schools further extended instructional time by providing tutoring in very small groups (one to five students) for students who were still struggling to learn the content after the initial core instruction. For example, after the first few years of its reform, Kennewick provided additional help to struggling students in the afternoon instead of placing those students' in an elective class, specifically on the basis of the theory that the greater the ALT for reading, the more likely it would be for struggling students to learn to proficiency. Since Kennewick had made reading proficiency the highest priority for the district, they were comfortable with reducing time for elective classes for those students who were struggling to read proficiently and could benefit from extra reading instruction in the afternoon.

Reducing Primary Grade Class Sizes to 15

Another strategy included in this section on using time more efficiently is lowering class sizes to 15 students in Kindergarten through Grade 3. This was a strategy used by many elementary schools that doubled performance, and generally it is a costly strategy. Odden and Archibald (2009) describe how schools found the resources to fund this strategy.

Two main mechanisms have been proposed through which class-size-reduction effects may operate. Some have suggested that teachers may alter their instructional methods in smaller classes, making greater use of small groups, for example, or assigning more writing, or more complex work. However, several studies, including those tied to Project STAR, the

Tennessee experimental study most cite as the rationale for implementing the practice, have failed to find consistent teaching differences related to class size (see Betts & Shkolnik, 1999; Evertson & Randolph, 1989; Rice, 1999). A more likely operating mechanism is that students respond better to the same instruction in smaller classes. With fewer students per teacher, less time is needed for disciplinary matters and students may be more engaged (Betts & Shkolnik, 1999; Finn & Achilles, 1999; Finn, Pannozzo, & Achilles, 2003). Both are mechanisms that essentially increase ALT. Particularly in the early elementary grades, smaller classes facilitate the forming of social relationships among teachers, students, and their families that may be essential for school success.

If nothing else, this approach means teachers could provide more individualized instruction to a smaller number of students in their reading classroom, and it was somewhat easier to take the formative assessment data for a group of 15 students, compared to 20 or 25 students, and design a coherent instructional plan based on the results. But when combined with cross-age grouping by achievement level, it allowed for even more targeted teaching, because all students in each class would be on essentially the same reading level.

Though there is a loud debate across the country on both the costs and effects of reducing class size as a strategy for boosting performance, I am simply reporting that many of the schools studied did seek to implement this strategy. And there is some theory to suggest that it can be a strategy to enhance the effectiveness of gross instructional minutes.

Secondary Schools

Options for increasing the effectiveness of time in secondary schools could include moving to a six-period day and reducing electives and providing double periods for some core classes.

Adopting a Six-Period Day

Secondary schools, both junior high and high schools, also altered how they used time during the regular school day. Unfortunately, the studies found no examples of secondary schools that increased the number of minutes in each period by reducing the number of periods in the day. However, this is an option I would recommend in the future; such a strategy would increase time for core subjects as well as lower overall school costs. Let me explain this assertion.

In the distant past (like when I was in junior and senior high school) but also still the case for some secondary schools in the country, the school day was divided into six periods. The day was about 6.5 to 6.45 hours, six periods for instruction and 30 to 45 minutes for lunch. Generally, for each period there was about 55 minutes for instruction and five minutes or so for moving between periods. But under several rationales, few actually shown by research to enhance learning, the number of periods was increased to seven and sometimes eight in a day. In almost no instance was the overall length of the school day increased. This meant that the number of minutes for each period was reduced. So secondary schools in many states and districts across the country actually provide fewer instructional minutes today for core subjects than they did years ago; put differently, by increasing the number of periods in the school day, there has been a trend in the country over the past decades to actually reduce instructional time for core subjects in many if not most secondary schools. Asking whether this has been a smart strategy might be the first step for secondary schools in how to use time more effectively.

Further, as the number of periods increased, the cost per student also rose and with little if any discernable rise in student learning. For a six-period day—the standard of the past—each student needed 1.2 teacher positions for each period, because teachers typically taught for five of the six periods and had planning and preparation time for the sixth period. So assuming students were in six class-size periods a day, the school needed an allocation of 1.2 teachers for each student. When the school day was divided into seven periods, teachers generally still taught only five periods, so every pupil then needed 1.4 teachers in order to have a teacher for every period. The cost of the seven-period day increased by 0.2 teachers; further, most if not all the additional teachers taught noncore elective classes. So what has happened over the past decades in many secondary schools is that the country reduced minutes of instruction in all subjects, including core subjects, and increased costs—certainly not a prescription for improving productivity in core subjects. An eight-period day extended this practice; even fewer minutes were provided for each subject, and each student needed 1.6 teachers, rather than the old standard of 1.2.[2]

One suggestion this book makes for all secondary schools, especially now in tight budget times, is to rethink the number of periods in the day. For reasons of both good time allocations as well as cost, schools should consider reverting back to a six-period school day; it would provide more minutes for instruction in all subjects, especially core content subjects, and it would cost less, which combined would make the school day more effective as well as more efficient and productive.

Reducing Electives and Providing Double Periods for Some Core Classes

Many secondary schools doubling student performance provided students additional help in core academic subjects by reducing the elective classes for struggling students. For example, the Talent Development High

School, and other middle and high schools as well, including Park Middle School in Kennewick, provided struggling students with "double" periods of mathematics and reading—one period of regular instruction and a second period to provide more targeted assistance, usually with different instructional approaches. The second period of academic help was provided at the expense of an elective course, usually in art or music or career/technical education; the rationale was that the basic building blocks for learning in all areas were reading and mathematics and if a student needed more help in these subjects, providing that help was more important than providing the elective class. An important part of this strategy was ensuring that these double periods of reading and math instruction did not just offer students more of the same but rather were staffed with teachers skilled in additional instructional approaches for reaching students who did not understand the material the first time they encountered it.

See Table 6.1 for a summary of the strategies discussed above.

Extending Planning and Preparation Time for Collaborative Work

All the schools that doubled student performance had elective teachers and generally provided all teachers with at least one period of student-free time to be used for planning and preparation of curriculum and instructional strategies. But most of the schools did more than just provide this time.

Table 6.1   Strategies for Better Uses of Time in Elementary and Secondary Schools

Strategies for Better Uses of Time in Elementary Schools	
• Protecting instructional time for core subjects • Extending time for some subjects • Maximizing effective use of instructional time • More time for struggling students • Reducing Class Size to 15 for Grades K–3	• Math and reading time free from interruptions • 90–120 minutes/day for reading • Multiage groupings based on abilities • Small-group/whole-group instruction • Small-group tutoring • More engagement • Fewer discipline issues • More use of small groups • Facilitation of social relationships
Strategies for Better Uses of Time in Secondary Schools	
• Adopting a six-period day • Reducing electives and providing double periods for core classes	• Increases time for core subjects • Lowers overall school costs • Double periods in math and reading (1/2 instruction; 1/2 extra help)

They then increased this time and scheduled it more effectively, thereby enabling teaches to implement a variety of collaborative strategies, including data-based decision making to improve instructional practice and multiple other actions to help create collaborative school cultures. These strategies are discussed in other chapters in this book. This section describes how the schools "maximized" time for these collaborative activities, drawing on Odden and Archibald (2009).

First, many schools scheduled all teachers on the same teams for the same pupil-free period. This included teams of grade-level teachers in elementary schools, and teams of content teachers in secondary schools. This allowed the teachers to meet and engage in various activities as a team. Some of the scheduling was incredibly creative for schools where teachers were part of two or three different decision-making teams. Grade-level teacher teams might be scheduled for common planning time two days a week. Then content teams (math, science) might be scheduled for a common time a third day, leaving time for other teams to be scheduled for common time the other two days. Further, the most effective schools were very clear that the agendas for each team had to be attended to, thus not letting student discipline problems or other subjects dominate all of the team meetings.

In some cases, when time for grade-level team meetings was not a part of the school schedules, other arrangements were made to ensure that teachers had this important time to collaborate. For example, in Monroe, Wisconsin, district leaders knew that having adopted a new math curriculum, an essential piece of ongoing professional development was regularly scheduled grade-level team meetings for teachers that totaled two hours per month. Since the teacher contract did not include time that could be used for such purposes, district leaders decided to pay teachers an additional stipend to ensure that teacher meetings around instruction took place. After the first year of implementation of the new math curriculum, each building principal built collaboration time into the school day. The amount of collaboration time varied by grade level and building, but the intent was to continue discussing how to best meet the needs of all the students.

Strategies to Provide More Collaborative Time During the Day

Second, schools devised many other strategies to provide teachers more time for collaboration during the regular school day. One common strategy was to have teachers extend the school day for 30 minutes for four days, and then release the students for 2 hours in the afternoon of the fifth day, which provided an extended time period for planning, professional development, and collaborative work to improve instructional practice. This type of strategy requires parent sanction and cooperation from the district, especially in situations where students are bussed to and from school. It nevertheless is a strategy widely used across the country—and it does not require additional resources. This approach provides all teachers two hours of uninterrupted planning time once every week, and at no additional fiscal cost.

Madison, Wisconsin, has implemented this strategy for years, releasing elementary teachers from instruction for about two hours every Monday but has not lengthened the school day for the other four days of the year. In this way, the district provides schools two hours of potential collaboration time one day of every week, in addition to the regular planning and preparation time periods.

Another strategy is to have teachers voluntarily begin school an hour before students arrive or remain at school for an hour after students leave. Yes, this represents additional time, but the teachers in such schools simply said that the job they wanted to accomplish required this extra time. Even though they might have a pupil-free period each day, and sometimes even a pupil-free afternoon, they said the ambitious restructuring they were involved in could not be done within that time constraint. This willingness to spend extra time collaborating on curriculum, instruction, and data-based decision making also suggested that teachers saw real value in spending their time in these activities; it helped them to be better and more focused in their classroom instructional activities.

Some schools devised even more creative ways to carve out the time teachers needed for collaborative work. One high school did two things that provided significant teacher planning and preparation time. First, students had a block of free time each day to engage in extended self-directed study. During these study times, they were not supervised by a licensed teacher. Second, students in the same school were required to perform service activities and engage in learning activities off the school campus in different locations around the community. Again, not all these ventures were directly supervised by a licensed teacher. Both of these components of the instructional program released teachers from instructional responsibilities and provided time for them to engage in planning, preparation, and professional development. This additional time was especially necessary because this school was implementing a complex integrated curriculum program that required this type of intensive planning. Therefore, by finding a way to provide these extensive time blocks to teachers, the school did what it needed to do to implement their new curricular strategy.

Another elementary school in an urban midwestern city set a goal to provide 90 minutes of uninterrupted planning time for each teacher team four days each week. This district is not a high-spending district, so the goal was ambitious. Moreover, the school also increased student instructional time, making the scheduling of the 90-minute planning time even more complex. An explanation of how the school planned to provide this preparation time follows.

First, prior to the new plan, students were scheduled for classes for six hours each day while teachers were scheduled for seven hours. This structure provided 60 minutes of free time each day for teachers. This time, combined with a planning period during the day, could have provided the time for the 90-minute planning block with some creative scheduling. But the school did not choose to do this because part of their new educational strategy was to extend the students' instructional time by one hour per day. To provide the additional hour of instruction, the school changed the student schedule to 8:00 a.m. to 3:00 p.m., the same as the teachers, thus eliminating that built-in hour of preparation time.

Next, the school set aside 8:00 a.m. to 1:00 p.m. as an uninterrupted *academic* instructional block each day. Instruction in reading, mathematics, science, and social studies was provided during these five hours. Teachers and students then had lunch from 1:00 to 1:30 p.m. After that, all classroom teachers had 90 minutes of planning time from 1:30 to 3:00 p.m. The most creative part of the schedule was how the school planned to provide this free time for all classroom teachers each afternoon.

The school took three full-time specialist teacher positions, which was part of its regular budget, and converted them into 10 part-time positions at 0.3 FTE (full-time equivalency) for each part-time position. The plan was to have the 10 part-time teachers provide all the supervision and instruction during the afternoon time from 1:00 to 3:00 p.m. In addition, because a teacher at 0.3 FTE works for two hours and 15 minutes per day, these teachers were also in charge of making sure students got on the busses between 3:00 and 3:15 p.m.

Of course, it does not work for both the teachers and the students to begin their day at 8 a.m., so the school required teachers to arrive at 7:45 a.m. instead. The school then compensated teachers for that extra time by allowing teachers to leave at 1:45 on Friday afternoons, while still allowing them the four 90-minute blocks of planning time each week.

However, the school was unable to implement the plan fully because they could not find the 10 part-time teachers. Nevertheless, the plan shows how it might be possible for a school to provide these large amounts of planning time but also extend the student's instructional time by an hour each day—without spending additional money.

Another elementary school in a large midwestern city wanted to provide a 90-minute planning block to each grade level five days each week. Their strategy was to schedule the normal planning period either right before or right after the teacher's lunch time. Though this required teachers to eat lunch during their 90-minute planning block, the teachers decided that this was a small price to pay for the benefit of a very long, uninterrupted block of planning time.

But as was the case with the other school that tried to schedule 90-minute blocks of planning time, this school was not able to implement this schedule for a number of reasons. First, if specialist time for each grade level was provided at the same time each day, the plan would allow only two grade levels to have the common planning time backed up with lunch— one grade with the specialists covering their classes before lunch and another after lunch. Second, if the grade levels were to rotate having specials backed up with lunch, the school could not meet the goal of providing five 90-minute blocks of planning time for every grade level each week.

Therefore, the school had to compromise its original goal and implement a plan that provided each grade level at least one 90-minute block of planning time a week, with a specialist covering one of the two periods backed up with the teachers' lunch. This strategy, however, required each grade to have specials classes at different times each day during the week. Initially, this was viewed as problematic because teachers felt elementary students liked and needed a consistent daily schedule. But as the plan was implemented, the school discovered that students were easily able to handle the differing daily schedule.

Another school in the same district was able to implement a 90-minute planning period backed up with lunch for each grade level by scheduling lunch at different times for different grade levels as follows:

Table 6.2 Staggered Lunch Schedule for Allocation of Extra Planning Time

Grade Level	Lunch Period	Planning Period
K–1	11:05–11:45 a.m.	11:50–12:35 p.m.
2–3	11:50 a.m.–12:35 p.m.	12:40–1:20 p.m.
4–5	12:40–1:20 p.m.	1:20–2:10 p.m.

In this way, every grade was able to have a 90-minute planning period when teachers decided to use lunch for this purpose.

It should be noted that the latter two examples are derived from research conducted by Karen Hawley Miles, and that the district was a strong union district. Further, teachers in the school proposed this schedule and use of lunch, which was beyond what was required by their union contract. But the teachers placed a high priority on long, uninterrupted planning periods and were able to find the time by using free time and specialist-provided time creatively.

In short, schools devised numerous strategies to provide significant time periods for planning, preparation, and professional development.

Box 6.1 includes a brief summary of the strategies for extending planning time for collaborative work.

Box 6.1   Strategies for Extending Planning and Preparation Time for Collaborative Work

- Schedule all teachers on the same teams for student-free periods.
- Schedule grade-level teacher teams for common planning two times per week.
- Extend the school day for 30 minutes for four days and release the students for 2 hours in the afternoon of the fifth day. Use the extra time for planning.
- Have teachers voluntarily begin school an hour before students arrive or remain at school for an hour after students leave.
- Give students a block of free time each day to engage in extended, self-directed study. Use this free time for planning.
- Have students participate in off-site service activities. Use the extra time for planning.
- Hire part-time teachers/specialists to provide supervision and instruction during one block of the day. Use the extra time for planning.
- Schedule lunch at different times for different grade levels so that schedules are staggered and more planning time can be built in.

In all the instances we have studied so far, faculties were helped in this creative process by having specialist staff already included in the regular school budget; these positions provided at least one period (30 to 55 minutes) of planning time each day during the week. And through creative scheduling, teachers were often able to find even more time for these important tasks. When asked whether it was worthwhile to give up their lunch period, nearly all teachers said some version of, "Yes, this does represent my having to use time for planning that was previously a free period, but the time expenditure is worth it because it has helped us in our collaborative work to improve our instructional strategies in ways that significantly increase student performance."

3. SUMMARY

Not everyone will agree with all the strategies implemented by these schools to use time during the school day in different and, what was for them, more effective ways. The schools and districts did not extend the school day or year. The point of this step is that those schools and districts took what was a "fixed" resource—the six hours of instruction during the regular school day—and created multiple strategies for using that time better, including class-size reduction at least in elementary schools. The strategies all allowed schools to increase academic learning time for the core academic subjects. By implementing these essentially no-cost time-use strategies schools used a resource more efficiently, because the fixed resource now was used to produce a higher level of student achievement outcomes. The examples show that schools and districts, even being educational organizations, can think of doing business in more efficient ways.

Unfortunately, the studies did not find any examples of schools that reduced seven- or eight-period days back to six-period days, thus reducing costs and increasing instructional time in core subjects, but this should be a strategy schools consider in the future.

Schools also devised a variety of different and often ingenious ways to increase collaborative planning and instructional work time for teachers, oftentimes creating 90 to 120 minute blocks of time for this work at least once or twice during the typical school week.

Readers are encouraged to continue to explore other ways to use school time more effectively. In a recent article in *Phi Delta Kappan,* Crawford (2008) argues that by involving teachers and principals in designing better ways to use time, education systems can identify multiple new strategies for reallocating school time in ways better for students and supported by teachers—without increasing costs.

Readers who work in secondary schools with seven- and eight-period days are especially encouraged to rethink this expensive approach to providing fewer minutes per instructional period; in a period of tight budgets, it might be time to revert back to a six-period day, which would both increase instructional minutes for core secondary school subjects and decrease school costs as well, a double benefit in tough times.

NOTES

1. It should be noted that most of those countries also teach all students today, not just those in the top achievement tiers, and that the student sample for the international comparisons of performance represents nearly all students, not just the top students. The Education Trust (see www.edtrust.org) also shows that the other countries' highest-performing students also outperform the highest-performing students in this country, so the reason for different performance levels is not due to student selection.

2. To be sure, some high school classes, such as physical education and band, might have large numbers of students but they are often offset by very small classes for advanced subjects like calculus or Spanish 4, so the discussion in the text of average classes still holds.

Extend Learning Time for Struggling Students[1]

The seventh strategy in the process of doubling student performance is providing multiple extra-help strategies for students struggling to learn to rigorous performance standards. All the elements of the steps that precede this step are crucial: (1) high achievement goals for all students; (2) consistent instructional practice and curriculum coverage in all classrooms; (3) the most effective instructional practice emanating from analysis of formative assessments, standards-based curriculum units and increasingly common end-of-unit assessments; (4) intensive, continuous, and ongoing professional development; (5) more efficient use of time during the school day; (6) professional communities that support high expectations, a systemic approach to instructional practice, collaborative teaching of curriculum content, and relentless pursuit of high performance for all children; and (7) professionals taking responsibility for the student achievement results of the school. Many readers might think this would be enough. But it is not.

No matter how good and powerful core instructional practice is, most schools will have some students (schools with high concentrations of students from lower-income backgrounds will have many) that need more than the instruction that is provided by the regular teacher to all students. Put differently, all classes will have students who struggle to learn to rigorous proficiency standards even when the best instructional practice is initially provided. To achieve to the performance standards required, these students need extra help; without extra help, it is unlikely that they will perform to standards.

All districts and schools that have doubled student performance and reduced the achievement gap provided multiple extra-help strategies for students struggling to achieve to proficiency or even higher performance standards. These extra supports reflect a strong American value of giving multiple opportunities for its citizens to accomplish certain goals—in this case, learning to a rigorous performance standard. The extra-help strategies are also supported by funds from categorical programs focused on struggling students, such as the federal Title 1 program (which is the generic title for the No Child Left Behind program) and similar state programs targeted to districts and schools with students from poverty backgrounds, students with disabilities, students whose native language is not English who must learn content as well as a new language—English—as they move through the education system, and so on. Depending on the state, there might be anywhere from a dozen to scores of such categorical program funding, which often can be pooled together (when districts seek permission to do so) to deliver the kinds of systemic extra-help strategies provided by the schools and districts making dramatic improvements in student learning.

Though these multiple funding streams can also complicate a cohesive approach to providing extra-help strategies and even in combination are not always adequate in many localities, the point is that both the federal and state governments provide funds through many, many programs for districts and schools to provide extra-help assistance to struggling students, putting their "money where their mouth is" to back the claim of federal, state, and local leaders that all children can learn to high standards. Odden and Archibald (2009) describe how many of the ways these funds had been used previously were dropped and the funds reallocated to the strategies described in this book and this chapter.

Furthermore, these extra-help strategies also reflect a long-recognized theory about learning—namely, that given sufficient time, most students can learn to reasonably high standards (Bransford, Brown, & Cocking, 1999; Cunningham & Allington, 1994; Donovan & Bransford, 2005a, 2005b, 2005c). The combined strategies described in this chapter represent the concrete ways these places varied (i.e., extended) learning time but held performance standards constant. The goal of all extra-help strategies was to expand learning and instructional time in ways that provided extra assistance to struggling students so that over time they could achieve to proficiency levels.

SOME CONTEXTUAL POINTS

Recall from the previous chapter that schools and districts often increased time during the regular school day for what they considered to be the most important subjects, such as reading and writing, mathematics, and increasingly, science, as the latter subject is now becoming a tested subject and part of accountability systems. Further, that core instructional time was protected from external interruptions so that the bulk of it was used for providing instruction to all students. All the additional services that are addressed in this chapter are in addition to this core instructional time, which in many cases was both lengthened and protected.

In addition, many of the interventions provided by the schools and districts doubling performance were done in the broad context of "response to intervention" though few districts actually used that phrase. Without getting into formal definitions of response to intervention, which is subject to intense debate across the country, the extra-help strategies provided aligned well with this general concept. See the different "tiers" of intervention in Box 7.1.

Box 7.1   Extra-Help Strategies

1. The first step is to provide high-quality instruction to all students, which is then followed by a tiered "continuum of extra services" and "differentiated instruction." This means that all students struggling to learn to proficiency standards as well as students with disabilities (except perhaps those with the most severe and profound disabilities) are taught first in the regular class-room, thus receiving high-quality instruction in the regular curriculum pro-vided by the regular classroom teacher. If a student has a mild struggle, the regular teacher then offers some within-class extra help, such as a small group that receives extra instruction a few times during the week, a multiplication table for a student with math problems, or other similar strategies.

2. The next "tier" of intervention is more intensive. It might be provided within the regular classroom or in a pull-out setting. This tier of intervention includes some combination of individual or small-group (maximum of five students) tutoring provided by a licensed teacher. In some cases, this tutoring is provided by a trained and supervised instructional aide, but rarely do trained aides tutor the students with the most complex learning challenges; that training is left to the expertise of a licensed and sometimes specially trained teacher. The second tier of intervention might also include an additional teacher working side-by-side with the regular teacher in the regular classroom, to provide a series of continu-ous extra help for students who need that assistance.

3. The next set of interventions include additional instructional time provided through some combination of "extended-day" (after school, before school, Saturday school, and so on) and/or summer school for students who, after receiv-ing the aforementioned extra services within the regular school day, still need extra help to learn to a proficiency level. The exact combination of extended-day and summer-school services, as well as the structure of these services, varies.

4. The final stage in the response to intervention approach is to provide even more additional services under the federal and state programs geared to students with identified disabilities, but all the previous services are options to be provided before a student is put into a program specifically geared to a disability.

The remainder of this chapter describes the variety of these extra-help strategies, organized by the nature of the extra time provided. Section 1 discusses extra help and time provided during the regular school day and year. Section 2 describes extra time and assistance provided outside the regular school day but within the regular school year. And Section 3 discusses the extra help, and thus extra instructional time, provided outside the regular school year. It should be noted that all "extra-help" and thus "extra-time" strategies reflect many of the recommendations of the Commission on Time and Student Learning and a recent report from the Education Sector (Silva, 2007).

1. TIME DURING THE REGULAR SCHOOL DAY

The most intensive extra-help strategy provided during the regular school day is tutoring, a strategy commonly viewed as "desired" but too expensive to consider realistically. Nevertheless, nearly all schools at all levels provided some combination of individual and small-group tutoring during the regular school day. Indeed, research shows that individual and very-small-group tutoring is one of the most effective—as well as resource intensive—extra-help strategies (Cohen, Kulik, & Kulik, 1982; Cohen, Raudenbush, & Ball, 2002; Mathes & Fuchs, 1994; Shanahan, 1998; Shanahan & Barr, 1995; Torgeson, 2004; Wasik & Slavin, 1993). The strategy is to intervene very quickly for students struggling over some concept in reading or mathematics and to provide intensive additional help so that the student learns the concept, rather than waiting and providing a remedial program after performance has dropped. Thus, the first extra-help strategy was one-to-one or other small-group tutoring but not for a group larger than five students. In most cases, the tutors were certified teachers trained as experts in reading; in some cases, trained and supervised instructional aides were used but usually with struggling students in the middle range of achievement.

Such individual tutoring was a core initial extra help and extended-time strategy used by Madison, Wisconsin; Kennewick, Washington; Rosalia, Washington; and Monroe, Wisconsin, as well as in nearly all *Reading First* programs, funded with a combination of reallocated resources as well as grants. It should be noted that there are many types of specific tutoring strategies, with varying costs, but Wasik and Slavin (1993) have documented impacts for *Reading Recovery, Success for All,* the *Wallach Tutoring* program, *Prevention of Learning Disabilities,* and *Programmed Tutorial Reading,* all of which use teachers as the tutors.

However, Farkas (1998) showed that if paraprofessionals (instructional aides) are selected according to clear and rigorous literacy criteria, trained in a specific reading-tutoring program, used to provide individual tutoring to students in reading, and are supervised, then they can have a significant impact on student reading attainment. Some districts have used Farkas-type tutors for students still struggling in reading in the upper-elementary grades. A study by Miller (2003) also showed that such aides could have an impact on reading achievement if used to provide individual tutoring to struggling students in the first grade.

Research on Tutoring

There is theory behind why individual one-to-one tutoring as well as very small-group tutoring boosts student learning. First, tutoring intervenes immediately when a student is trying to learn. Second, tutoring is explicitly tied to the specific learning problem evidenced. Third, when provided by a trained professional, tutoring offers the precise and appropriate substantive help the student needs to overcome the learning challenge. Fourth, tutoring should thus remedy short-term learning problems and in many cases is not to be needed on a continuing basis. In short, though potentially expensive, the ability of tutoring to intervene quickly, precisely, and effectively to undo an individual's specific learning challenge gives it the potential to have a large effect, particularly when the specific learning challenge or challenges are key concepts related to a student's learning the grade-level expectations for a content area.

However, the impact of tutoring programs depends on how they are structured. The alignment between what a tutor does and the regular instructional program is important and the more aligned, the greater the impact (Mantzicopoulos, Morrison, Stone, & Setrakian, 1992; Wheldall, Coleman, Wenban-Smith, Morgan, & Quance, 1995). Who conducts the tutoring matters, as does the intensity of the tutoring. Indeed, certified teacher tutors have more impact than paraprofessionals as tutors (Shanahan, 1998). Poorly organized programs in which students lose instructional time moving between classrooms can limit tutoring effects (Cunningham & Allington, 1994). Analysts (Cohen et al., 1982; Farkas, 1998; Gordon, 2009; Mathes & Fuchs, 1994; Shanahan, 1998; Shanahan & Barr, 1995; Wasik & Slavin, 1993) have found greater effects when the tutoring includes the following mechanisms:

- Professional teachers as tutors
- Tutoring initially provided to students on a one-to-one basis
- Tutors trained in specific tutoring strategies
- Tutoring tightly aligned to the regular curriculum and to the specific learning challenges, with appropriate content-specific scaffolding and modeling

- Sufficient time provided for the tutoring
- Highly structured programming, both substantively and organizationally

An important issue is how many tutors to provide for schools with differing numbers of at-risk students. The standard of many comprehensive school designs is a ratio of one fully licensed teacher-tutor for every 100 at-risk students, usually defined as the number of students from a low-income or poverty background, with a minimum of one for every school. This provision standard would provide from one to four professional teacher-tutor positions for the typical all-poverty 400-student elementary and middle schools. Gordon (2009) notes that Finland, one of the countries now recognized as having the highest-performing students as well as a highly effective way of staffing schools, provides about one specially trained tutor for every seven classroom teachers. In the U.S. context, for a four-section, K–5 elementary school with 20 students in each classroom (so therefore 24 regular teachers), this formula would provide about three full-time tutor positions, regardless of poverty level. If elective teachers for art, music, and physical education were counted, the formula would provide four tutor positions to the school.

The specific structural features of one-to-one tutoring strategies varied by school and district. For some, each tutor would tutor one student every 20 minutes, or three students per hour. This would allow one tutor position to tutor 18 students a day. (Since tutoring is such an intensive activity individual teachers might spend only half their time tutoring; but a 1.0 FTE tutoring position would allow 18 students per day to receive one-to-one tutoring.) Four positions would allow 72 students to receive individual tutoring daily in an all-poverty 400-student elementary and middle school. However, since most students do not require tutoring all year long, the bulk of the tutoring programs generally assess students quarterly and change tutoring arrangements. With modest changes such as these, close to half the student body of a 400-pupil school unit could receive individual tutoring during the year. Third, not all students who are from a low-income background require individual tutoring, so a portion of the tutoring time might be used for students in the school who might not be from a lower-income family but nevertheless have a learning issue that could be remedied by tutoring.

Though schools initially emphasized *individual* tutoring, schools also deployed tutoring resources in evidence-based ways other than just individual tutoring. In a detailed review of the evidence on how to structure a variety of early intervention supports to prevent reading failure, Torgeson (2004) shows, based on studies when different tutoring configurations were tried on a randomized basis, how one-to-one tutoring, one-to-three tutoring, and one-to-five small-group sessions can be combined for different students to enhance their chances of learning to read successfully. One-to-one tutoring would be reserved for the students with the most severe reading difficulties, scoring, say, at or below the twentieth or twenty-fifth percentile on a norm-referenced test. Intensive instruction for groups of three to five students would then be provided for students above that level but below the proficiency level.

The instruction for all groupings of elementary students, though, needs to be more explicit and sequenced than that for other students. Young children with weaknesses in knowledge of letters, letter-sound relationships, and phonemic awareness need explicit and systematic instruction to help them first decode and then learn to read and compre-hend (see Torgeson, 2004, for details).

Torgeson (2004) further shows that meta-analyses consistently show the positive effects of reducing reading-group size (Elbaum, Vaughn, Hughes, & Moody, 1999) and identifies experiments with both one-to-three and one-to-five teacher-student groupings. While one-to-one tutor-ing works with 20 minutes of tutoring per student, a one-to-three or one-to-five grouping requires a longer instructional time for the small group of up to 45 minutes. The two latter groupings, with 45 minutes of instruction, reduced the rate of reading failure to a miniscule percentage.

Following these recommendations, a one FTE reading position could teach 30 students a day in the one-to-three setting with 30 minutes of instruction per group, and 30 or more students a day in the one-to-five setting with 45 minutes of instruction per group. Four FTE tutoring posi-tions could then provide this type of intensive instruction for up to 120 students daily. In short, while one-to-one tutoring is the most intensive intervention and generally was used for struggling students in the bottom quarter or third of the achievement range, other small-group practices also were used, with the length of instruction for the small group increas-ing as the size of the group increases. The interventions only help ele-mentary students learn to read if they provide the type of explicit instruction described by Torgeson (2004).

Although Torgeson (2004) states that similar interventions can work with middle and high school students, the effect, unfortunately, is smaller, as it is much more difficult to undo the lasting damage of not learning to read when students enter middle and high schools with severe reading deficiencies.

Approaches for Secondary Students

Although there were a few instances when middle and high schools also provided tutoring for some students, the general approach to providing extra help during the regular school day for secondary students was different. The primary approach for middle and high schools was to provide double periods for students struggling generally in mathematics or reading/language arts. Indeed, in most of the middle and high schools, reading was provided as a separate subject in addition to a language arts class because large numbers of students entered school reading below grade level. Most of these schools also initiated a "reading across the curriculum" approach that had every subject-area teacher emphasizing the vocabulary and reading skills needed for their specific subject.

What Time Does Tutoring Replace?

The reader might wonder what subject was replaced by the tutoring in elementary schools or the extra reading or math or science class in secondary schools. The answer is some elective, such as art, music, health, career and technical education, and so on. Though all schools and districts wanted all their students to have a broad-based "liberal arts" education, they concluded that if a student entered secondary school with deficiencies in reading or mathematics skills, they simply had to address those deficiencies in order for that student to be successful in any content class. Thus, they provided extra help during some elective period: The extra reading, mathematics, science, or tutoring during that class period was deemed more important for the long-term success of the students than an elective class. Because these schools and districts had made student performance in the core subjects—reading, writing, mathematics, science, history, and world language—the prime goals of the schools, it was easier for them to make a difficult decision about how to use the fixed resource of time: Performing to standards in core subjects was the first priority, so if performance was lagging, time was taken from other subjects to provide the extra help during the regular day to ensure performance in core subjects.[2]

2. TIME OUTSIDE THE REGULAR SCHOOL DAY BUT WITHIN THE REGULAR SCHOOL YEAR

The second kind of extra-help and extra-time strategy was academic help provided for the time periods before school, after school, and in Saturday school programs. Columbus Elementary School in Appleton actually obtained a *Twenty-First Century* school grant to fund this strategy. Sometimes the programs provided individual tutoring during these time periods, and other times the programs provided more general homework help.

The specific organization of the extra help for this extended-day strategy varied across nearly all schools and districts. Some schools provided two hours of extended-day programming after schools, and some just an hour. Sometimes licensed teachers provided the academic help portion of the program, and in other cases that help was provided by paraprofessionals, some trained and some not that trained. The same was true for academic help provided in the hour before school started and in Saturday schools.

It also should be noted that these approaches faced challenges that no school or district has resolved to their satisfaction. Many times, students who needed the help did not attend the program, and lack of attendance and participation clearly diminished the impact of these strategies.

Though the specific structure of the extended-day academic assistance varied considerably, it was a component of the extra-help strategies in most of the sites doubling student performance.

Research on Extended-Day Programs

Several developmental theories have been used to understand how effective afterschool programs work (Vandell, Pierce, & Dadisman, 2005). Using these theoretical frames applied to various programs that have been studied and focusing on the developmental and learning needs of children and adolescents, Vandell and her associates identified positive relationships between program staff and students, rich content-based program activities, and learning- and mastery-oriented content delivery strategies as the major features of effective after school and extended-day programs. A widely referenced review of extended-day and after school programs identifies academic, recreational, and cultural components of an effective after school program with an emphasis on training staff for effective implementation (Fashola, 1998). Though there are still many outstanding questions about how to make extended-day programs more effective, researchers identified several structural and institutional supports necessary for effective after school programs, including the following:

- Staff qualifications and support (staff training in child or adolescent development, after school programming, elementary or secondary education, and content areas offered in the program; staff expertise; staff stability/turnover; compensation; and institutional supports)
- Program/group size and configuration (enrollment size, ages served, group size, age groupings, and child-staff ratio)
- Financial resources and budget (dedicated space and facilities that support skill development and mastery, equipment and materials to promote skill development and mastery, curricular resources in relevant content areas, and location that is accessible to youth and families)

- Program partnerships and connections (with schools to connect administrators, teachers, and programs; with larger networks of programs; and with parents and community)
- Program sustainability strategies (institutional partners, networks, linkages; community linkages that support enhanced services; long-term alliances to ensure long-term funding)

Though there is no independent assessment of the specific impact of extended-day programs and strategies in the schools and districts that doubled performance, the fact is that most of them provided some level of extended-day programming focused on either providing tutoring or some kind of homework help as part of their overall portfolio of strategies to extend learning and instructional time for struggling students.

3. TIME OUTSIDE THE REGULAR SCHOOL YEAR

Finally, the last extra-help strategy was summer school, a strategy that research shows to be effective if it has a clear academic focus such as reading and mathematics instruction for elementary and middle school students, and retaking high school courses failed during the regular school year for high school students (Borman & Boulay, 2004; Borman, Rachuba, Hewes, Boulay, & Kaplan, 2001; Cooper, Charlton, Valentine, & Muhlenbruck, 2000). The various schools and districts funded this strategy with a combination of reallocated funds and new grants or through existing state support for summer school programming.

The approaches to summer school also varied radically, with almost no clear common element. Summer programs ranged from four to eight weeks; some were half- and some full-day programs; most had some academic emphasis for part of the day, but the amount of summer school time strictly devoted to academics varied widely. Again, there is no independent assessment of the effect of summer school programming per se for the districts and schools studied but like extended-day programming it was among the portfolio of extended-time strategies that were provided.

Research on Summer School Programming

Research dating back to 1906 shows that students, *on average*, lose a little more than a month's worth of skill or knowledge over the summer break (Cooper, Nye, Charlton, Lindsay, & Greathouse, 1996). Summer breaks have a larger negative impact on at-risk (poverty background) children's reading and mathematics achievement, which falls further over the summer break than for middle-class students. This loss can reach as much as one-third of the learning during a regular nine-month school year (Cooper et al., 1996). A longitudinal study, moreover, showed that these family-income-based summer learning differences *accumulate* over the elementary school years, such that poor children's achievement scores without summer school fall further and further behind the scores of middle-class students as they progress through school grade by grade (Alexander & Entwisle, 1996). As a result of this research, there is emerging consensus that what happens during the summer can significantly impact the achievement of students from low-income and at-risk backgrounds (see also Heyns, 1978).

Evidence on the effectiveness of summer programs in attaining these positive goals, however, typically is sparse because research reviews have drawn from research on high-, medium-, and low-quality summer school programs. Although past research linking student achievement to summer programs shows only some promise for the effectiveness of such programs, several studies suffer from methodological shortcomings and the low quality of the summer school programs themselves.

However, a relatively recent meta-analysis of 93 summer school programs (Cooper et al., 2000) found that the average student in summer programs outperformed about 56 to 60% of similar students not receiving the programs, though only a small number of studies (e.g., Borman et al., 2001) used random assignment, and program quality varied substantially.

Nevertheless, evidence from research generally suggests that summer school is needed and can be effective for at-risk students. Studies suggest that the effects of summer school are largest for elementary students when the programs emphasize reading and mathematics and for high school students when programs focus on courses students failed during the school year. For example, using a randomized sample of 325 students who participated in the Voyager summer school program, research found that these students showed gains in reading achievement, with an effect size of 0.42 (Roberts, 2000). The more modest effects frequently found in middle school programs can be partially explained by the emphasis in many middle school summer school programs on adolescent development and self-efficacy rather than on academics.

Ascher (1988); Austin, Roger, and Walbesser (1972); and Heyns (1978) identified several programmatic characteristics that undercut program impacts and thus produced the modest effects research has documented so far. They include short program duration (sometimes a result of funding delays and late program start dates), loose organization, little time for advanced planning, low *academic* expectations for either mathematics or reading, discontinuity between the summer curriculum and the regular-school-year curriculum, teacher fatigue, and poor student attendance. On the other hand, in their meta-analysis of summer program effects, Cooper and colleagues (2000) noted several program components that are related to improved achievement effects for summer program attendees. These components are supported by the recommendations in the most recent book on summer school and how to enhance its impacts (Borman & Boulay, 2004):

- Early intervention during elementary school
- A full six- to eight-week summer program
- A clear focus on mathematics and reading achievement, or failed courses for high school students
- Small-group or individualized instruction
- Parent involvement and participation
- Careful scrutiny for treatment fidelity, including monitoring to ensure good instruction in reading and mathematics is being delivered
- Monitoring student attendance

Summer programs that include these elements hold the most promise for schools seeking to improve the achievement of at-risk students and close the achievement gap, which constituted the bulk of schools that have doubled student performance.

4. SUMMARY

Not all students received all the above types of extra-help and extended-learning opportunities, and not all districts and schools provided all of them. However, the schools and districts that have doubled performance offered a variety of combinations of double periods, tutoring, extended-day and summer school extra-help programs—all strategies that extended the learning time for students struggling to achieve to performance standards in core subjects but particularly in mathematics, reading, and writing. The point is that the places that doubled student performance had a rich set of extra-help strategies, all providing additional time with additional instructional support while maintaining the goal of having students achieve up to and beyond the proficient or advanced levels of performance. And providing this extra instructional time was a critical part of their overall efforts to dramatically boost student learning.

Because each of these interventions requires extra resources, schools and districts seeking to produce large gains in student achievement need a budget strategy to fund these extended-time initiatives. Odden and Archibald

(2009) describe multiple funding strategies, and Odden and Picus (2008) show how resources for these strategies can and should be incorporated into revised state school funding structures.

NOTES

1. The research sections of this chapter draw from Odden and Picus (2008).

2. Just to make the point, no research shows that students who would take an art or music course *instead* of these second extra-help classes do better in reading and mathematics. Although there is research that students who do well in music also do well in mathematics, the schools and districts doubling performance knew that a music class could not function as an extra-help class for a student struggling in mathematics; extra help and time focused on mathematics (or whatever subject in which the student was struggling) is needed to help get that student up to performance standards.

Collaborative Cultures and Distributed Leadership

The eighth strategy in the process of doubling student performance concerns something built inside the school or district. It is both something that can be structured as well as something that evolves from implementing the previous strategies, and that is creating a collaborative school culture with distributed leadership provided by both teachers and administrators. Given the collaborative and interactive nature of the work on curriculum and instruction indicated by the previous chapters of this book, which also includes teachers functioning in a variety of new leadership roles, it should be no surprise that one result of the multiplicity of activities was a collaborative professional school culture that included as one of its core features many teachers involved in a wide array of instructional leadership roles.

In many ways, this strong culture was largely a product of the multiple collaborative activities described in the previous chapters, not something created by the schools and districts *before* engaging in the processes to double student performance. However, because the schools and districts engaged in the doubling-performance processes in a collaborative fashion from Strategy 1, the leaders understood that the way to attain their ambitious goals was to proceed in a cooperative and not a bureaucratic manner, with the goal over time of developing a collaborative and professional school culture, what is commonly called a professional learning community today. Moreover, because the operation of the multiple collaborative groups needed coordination and leadership to make them work, a related result was creation of an impressive array of instructional leadership positions filled by individuals in nearly all roles (teacher, principal, central office staff) at the school and district levels.

This chapter first discusses the nature of the collaborative professional school cultures that were created and how they are very similar professional learning communities. Section 2 shows how school leaders can create school structures that facilitate the development of and support for collaborative cultures and professional learning communities. Section 3 describes how these collaborative approaches to running schools also produced widespread distributed leadership by teachers and administrators.

1. A COLLABORATIVE SCHOOL CULTURE

Education writing includes at least two strains of literature on the nature of effective school cultures. In the early 1990s, Newmann and associates (1996) defined what they called a "professional school culture," a concept that emerged from their studies of effective secondary schools—that is, secondary schools that had dramatically improved achievement and reduced the achievement gap in the process. The second strand has emerged more recently from the work of Rick and Becky DuFour and Doug Reeves, among others, on what they label professional learning communities, or PLCs. Both concepts generally refer to teams of teachers working together to improve the curriculum and instructional program in order to boost student learning. Both sanction the notion that schools with teachers working in isolation, no matter how good, are less effective than schools with teachers working together in teams, as has been described in many different ways in the examples given in the previous chapters. Indeed, seasoned experts on professional development geared to improving student performance, Shirley Hord and Stephanie Hirsh (2009) and Linda Darling-Hammond (Darling-Hammond & Richardson, 2009) argue that PLCs are the most powerful concept now for schools to improve their effectiveness.

The Newmann and associates (1996) concept of a professional school culture includes the following key notions:

- Teachers share high achievement expectations for all students.
- Teachers share common values such as relentless pursuit of high student performance.

- Instruction is "de-privatized" meaning it is public and openly discussed, with teachers often observing other teachers' instructional practice.
- Teachers take responsibility for the student performance results of their actions.

It should be clear that the schools and districts profiled in this book align strongly with this notion of a professional school culture.

The high expectations created in Strategy 2 reflect the first element. Indeed, in talking with teachers and principals in the schools that have doubled performance, it is clear that everyone holds very high expectations for student achievement, believes holding high expectations for such learning is a moral imperative, and is engaged in relentless pursuit of attaining those ambitious goals. Though teachers and administrators knew the goals were ambitious, they had been involved in setting them, they believed they could attain them, they believed that attaining them was the right thing to do, and they structured their work so as to move toward attaining those goals year after year.

The schools that doubled student performance shared common values of high expectations, collaborative work, moving from data to practice, and in many schools, the general notion that the school engaged in the "response to interventions" approach for struggling students to make sure that all students had maximum opportunities, supported by a set of differentiated strategies, to achieve to rigorous performance standards.

The development of a common approach to effective instruction, characteristic of virtually all schools and districts doubling performance, is the embodiment of the de-privatization of instruction. In the schools and districts doubling performance, instructional practice was not something that was individualistic and private to each teacher. The schools and districts worked collaboratively to create a common, schoolwide, systemic approach to good instructional practice; spent time observing each others' classrooms; had experts or instructional coaches assisting individual teachers to deploy new instructional practices in their classrooms; and used large portions of the collaborative discussions of the formative assessment data to determine collectively how to craft instructional units tailored to those data. As a result, instruction was something out in the open, as it were—the subject of public and professional conversations and the focus of ongoing professional development.

In districts like both Madison, Wisconsin, and Montgomery County, Maryland, the public nature of good instructional practice represented an enormous change from the status quo, but as previously described, the change was largely welcomed by teachers, who were hungry for detailed information about how to implement new instructional practices that were designed to attain the ambitious learning goals for all students. Indeed, in one elementary school in Montgomery County, the teachers interviewed said that they would not want in their schools teachers who would not engage in collaborative work or who would not work to help create curriculum units, simultaneously teach them, and then debrief on their effectiveness. That was the way teacher work in the school was defined and they wanted all teachers in the school to "buy into" that approach to instruction or to find a job elsewhere.

Finally, the last element of a professional culture—taking responsibility for student achievement results—means that faculties and administrators take credit for the student performance changes that were produced whether performance went up or down. When student performance rose, which happened in most schools over time, the faculties believed it was a result of their hard work on the curriculum and instructional program. Yes, it took student effort as well, but it was student effort that emerged from instructional units and experiences designed and implemented by the teachers in the school. Further, when performance did not rise, which did happen at various times in nearly all schools over the course of many years of overall improvement, the faculties went back to the drawing board to determine why and to decide what to change instructionally for that unit the next year.

An excellent example of this latter point was a side comment in the presentation of the principal of Elmont Junior-Senior High School at the 2007 Wisconsin Conference. He said that one year only 89% of the students passed the difficult New York State Geography Regents test and in the next breath said, "We obviously had done something wrong." These comments reflect two key points: The first is that the lower scores reflected a mistake the faculty made, not something about students, and the second is that an 89% passing rate was not good enough, which reinforced the very high performance expectations in the school.

The same was true in Aldine, Texas, when it discovered shortcomings in student achievement in mathematics and advanced language. The response to the data was to rethink the science and English-as-a-second-language strategies, believing that if the students were not doing well in these areas, then it was the curriculum and the instructional practice that was part of that curriculum that was the problem that needed to be fixed, not something about the students or their parents.

As these examples illustrate, the schools and districts doubling performance believed that all students could learn, and that their achievement was the result of hard work by teachers and principals on the instructional program. When performance did not match expectations, they did not say, "Oh, this group of ninth graders was not as smart as last year's."

They did not say, "Well, we need more money," or "We had to narrow the curriculum because of NCLB (No Child Left Behind) pressures," or "If we had more parent involvement, the kids would do better." They said *they* got something wrong in their curriculum and instructional program and then worked collaboratively to fix it. As a principal in Kennewick, Washington, described the process he puts in motion whenever data from the school's MAP testing reveals a problem with student performance, "I gather up the teachers in the affected grade, point out the problem, and assign them the task of coming up with a solution to be presented to all faculty during the next professional development day previously built into the school calendar."

Finally, it should go without saying that a professional culture includes dogged, relentless, and continuous pursuit of a high level of achievement and learning for all students. These staffs authentically work to leave no child behind. For example, Madison had a central-office staff person who reviewed the periodic running reading records of all students in the district and then, during school visits, asked the principal and teacher why certain students were not making progress; this is one example of an intense focus in these schools and districts of working to ensure that *each and every* student succeeded and no child fell through the cracks.

As another example, at Franklin Elementary School in Appleton, Wisconsin, when data revealed a weakness in student writing, the principal implemented a system that required teachers to submit a sample of writing from each student to the principal, who then personally reviewed each writing sample and approached the classroom teachers of students who were weak writers and made sure a plan was in place to address the problem.

The multiple extra-help strategies discussed in the previous chapter also reflect this relentless effort to have all students achieve: If the first dose of instruction did not work, then the school and its teachers provided a second, third, and even fourth dose in order to have as many students achieve to the high bars set for them.

PLCs as an Extension of the Notion of a Professional School Culture

It should be clear that the Dufour and others' notion of a PLC could also have been used to encapsulate the above concepts of the schools' culture (DuFour, DuFour, Eaker, & Many 2006). PLCs, moreover, are also associated today with the analysis of formative assessments by teacher teams, a phenomenon that has emerged more in the last decade than was present during the time of the Newman and associates (1996) research.

Moreover, as was the case in nearly all of the schools doubling performance, the collaborative analysis of formative and common end-of-unit assessment results by teachers in grade-level or content teams represent clear examples of PLCs in these schools. Because these schools have produced dramatic improvements in student achievement, they align quite well with the many research studies on the efficacy of PLCs as the context for teachers' collaboratively engaging in data-based decision making about curriculum and instruction (Black & Wiliam, 1998).

Moreover, the notion of PLCs should not be interpreted to mean some kind of "soft" set of teacher interactions. If one reads the work of the DuFours, who advocate for the notion of developing PLCs in all schools, one discovers that PLCs is a harder-core concept: PLCs are a means to produce much higher levels of student learning as well as an ongoing strategy to enhance teacher learning (DuFour et al., 2006). The operation of PLCs is quite similar to the work of teachers in Montgomery County: The goal is to dramatically improve student learning; the strategy is (1) to work collaboratively to analyze formative student data and create common instructional units with common end-of-unit tests, (2) to debrief on how the units went, and (3) to do this continuously through the school year with the pressure on themselves to attain the goal of dramatically improving student learning regardless of the demographic context or background of the students.

PLCs, moreover, stand in opposition to individualist work of teachers, just as argued in the professional development chapter. For PLCs to work, teachers need to share ideas (even if they are criticized), share thoughts about instructional practice (even if proven that they do not work), and be open to have the performance of their own students scrutinized by the members of the group or PLC (even if their own students are not performing very well), in addition to all the positives mentioned above. So PLCs also are meant to be forums in which difficult conversations occur— conversations that must occur in order for the instructional practice of all teachers to change and improve as the prime route to producing much higher levels of student learning.

As discussed in the professional development chapter, PLCs also function as powerful learning structures for teachers. By working together with other teachers and analyzing a variety of student performance data—both formative and summative—all teachers learn in an open and collaborative context how formative assessment data are connected to instructional practice, what works, what does not work, which teachers are effective and which are not, and how to improve curriculum and instruction approaches when initial strategies are not as successful as anticipated. As early as 1998, Black and Wiliam (1998) argued that the use of formative assessments in support of student learning development and in the context of professional learning communities, promises significant potential gains in student achievement, and a model of teacher professional development that can be implemented effectively at scale. The dozens of districts and schools doubling student performance today and using PLCs like this supports this decade-old claim.

In sum, all the schools and districts that doubled student performance produced professional, collaborative school cultures or PLCs over time. In these organizations, central-office staff, school administrators, and teachers all worked together to attain their ambitious student performance goals.

2. STRUCTURING COLLABORATIVE CULTURES

Although school cultures can represent a soft concept, something that is somewhat hard to grab hold of, rather than a hard concept such as a curriculum scope and sequence, for example, school leaders, including principals, assistant principals, and teacher leaders, can create structures and do other things to facilitate the operation of PLCs and the collaborative work of teacher teams.

One obvious act is to *create teacher teams* and have them led by teacher coordinators or leaders. A core set of teams would be the grade-level teachers in elementary schools and content-area teachers in secondary schools; such teams could be coordinated be a senior, effective teacher in that team. Indeed, the previous chapters referred to many examples of such teams. In Montgomery County, elementary schools also had teams of preschool and kindergarten teachers to help coordinate the preschool and regular elementary school program in schools that had preschool programs in them. All of these team examples would be called "horizontal" teams, because each member would be teaching the same content.

In other contexts, elementary schools also have content teams, such as math, reading, writing, or science teams, composed of teachers from different grade levels and again coordinated or led by a teacher. These would be called "vertical" teams, because they would be composed of teachers at different grade levels, each of whom would be teaching the same subject but at a different grade level.

There also could be a *schoolwide curriculum committee* composed of the teacher coordinators of each of the curriculum teams, as well as each of the coordinators of the grade-level teams. These teams often were chaired by teachers who were the instructional coaches or lead professional developer teachers in the school.

A similar rich structure of teacher teams can be created in secondary schools.

In addition to creating collaborative teacher teams, another key leadership role is to create a school schedule that ensures that teachers in each team have some *common free time during each week* so that the team can meet during the regular school day to plan and prepare. Given multiple teams, this scheduling task can become complicated, but nearly all the schools doubling performance scheduled teachers in the various teams at the same time so they could engage in collaborative work on the curriculum and instructional program during the regular school day. Moreover, for these teachers, planning and preparation was teamwork, not individual work, because they prepared curriculum units that they all would actually teach; it was collaborative work directly related to their teaching responsibilities. One resource to tap for how to schedule teachers with common time is www.allthingsPLC.info, under the Tools & Resources link. This Web site also provides examples of how PLCs in other schools and districts have improved student learning and has a mechanism for connecting with PLCs in other places around the country.

A third leadership role is to *provide training for both team leaders and coordinators* in how to run meetings where teachers do real work and make decisions. This training would cover how to create an agenda, run meetings according to the agenda, get teachers to make decisions, and develop a mechanism to monitor how decisions are implemented. There also is a need for training teachers in how to work effectively in teacher teams. Though both of these training foci might seem unnecessary, very few teachers have received training either in how to function in a work team such as a PLC or on how to lead or coordinate such a work team. Though this training need not go on forever, school leaders that provide this kind of training are rewarded with more effective PLCs in their schools.

In sum, to create reciprocal accountability in the school, both for the best instructional practice and high student performance, the school administration is responsible for providing the time, structures, training, materials, and encouragement that facilitate the work of teacher teams in PLCs. Conversely, teachers are then responsible for working in these contexts to use data on student performance to strengthen curriculum and instructional practice so that students learn to higher and higher levels year over year.

Put differently, neither collaborative cultures nor PLCs emerge spontaneously. Systems, structures, training, and other supports need to be provided to facilitate their work and these actions require initiative on the part of school administrators.

3. DISTRIBUTED LEADERSHIP

One not surprising result from the above school structures that helps to engage teachers in multiple and collaborative decision-making activities is strong instructional leadership provided not only by principals but also by teachers, as well as central-office staff. In the educational literature, this is often called distributed leadership (e.g., Spillane, 2006; Spillane, Halverson, & Diamond, 2001). What is clear from the districts and schools that have doubled performance, that I or colleagues of mine have studied, as well as those studied by others (e.g., Chenoweth, 2007), is that leadership emerges at all levels in the system, and it is the combined effect of this "distributed leadership" that helps improve instructional practice that produces the ambitiously high student performance results.

In some cases, schools can produce dramatic improvements in student learning on their own but it certainly is facilitated if there is support from the central office. Further, central-office leadership also is needed to move all schools in a district onto the pathway toward doubling student performance. The Kennewick case showed that not only central-office administrators but also board members visited each school to launch their process to have every student reading proficiently by the end of third grade. In Montgomery County, the whole change process was initiated by the superintendent, who not only facilitated all the moving parts of that district's collaborative reform efforts but also deployed central-office staff to help teacher teams map the district's curriculum standards to the state standards and then restructured the central budget so all schools received at least one professional development teacher whose specific role was to provide instructional leadership. Further, as in other districts, central-office individuals need to be involved both to ensure that state-level testing data were made available in a useable format to teachers and administrators in schools and to provide funds for resources schools need to implement their strategies (like the professional development teachers in Montgomery County), in addition to sometimes also providing the authority for schools to reallocate site resources for the needs of a new educational strategy.

At the school level, principals were usually unable to provide all the instructional leadership needed to change the entire curriculum, create and implement a professional development strategy, work with teachers on the analysis of formative assessment data, and provide the classroom coaching that teachers need to change their instructional practice. Thus, as indicated in the professional development chapter and the above sections on collaborative cultures, teachers were promoted into roles of team coordinator, instructional coach, curriculum head, induction mentor, or curriculum facilitator to expand, deepen, and intensify the instructional leadership that was provided at the school. Though the schools and districts had a wide variety of teacher instructional leadership roles, research is only beginning to show how formal and informal teacher leadership can be most effectively structured (Mangin & Stoelinga, 2008), although the writing on PLCs gives multiple examples of how teachers with teacher leaders can engage in a wide range of data-based decision making (DuFour et al., 2006).

In Abbotsford, Wisconsin, district and school leaders created an environment of shared decision making at the school level. Whether making decisions about curriculum adoption, scheduling, or class lists, a team of teachers was always involved. The principal believed that it should be natural and important to ask for teacher expertise whenever decisions are made. This philosophy of leadership had an impact on the school culture, creating an environment in which collaboration and conversation are encouraged and supported by the administration. Teachers are encouraged to take on leadership positions, helping one another with practice, deciding on new textbooks, and contributing to the design of the school reform. The open lines of communication and trust between faculty and administrators help the school make decisions as a community.

This and other examples in this and other books (Chenoweth, 2007; Odden & Archibald, 2009) show that many teachers in the districts and schools engaged in the process of doubling student performance became engaged in a wide range of instructional leadership activities, which provided them not only career advancement but also the opportunity to ensure that teachers were centrally involved in leading the curriculum and instructional changes that were the foundation of the overall strategy to dramatically boost student academic learning.

Though these findings reinforce the notion that principals in good schools are instructional leaders, it should be noted that the principal does not always have to be the person doing the instructional leadership activities. The function of managing the school—that is, scheduling students, dealing with parents, monitoring the budget, fixing the roof and broken toilets, ensuring security, and so on—has to be conducted by someone. If the principal does these tasks, then he or she needs to promote teachers into even stronger instructional leadership roles, which often was the case. On the other hand, if the principal wanted to spend the bulk of his or her time doing instructional leadership, then he or she needs to make sure some individual is responsible for the other, more mundane management aspects of the school, because both the instructional and noninstructional tasks need attention.

The prime conclusion for the schools and districts doubling performance is that there was a "density" of instructional leaders in these educational organizations: central-office individuals who often have the formal authority to lead the system, principals to lead and manage the site, and teachers as team leaders, instructional coaches, teacher mentors, grade-level or department-level team coordinators, and/or schoolwide instructional or curriculum facilitators. In part because of the widespread and distributed leadership structures, the result was that there was sufficient instructional leadership in the organization, the organization was able to maintain its course even when certain formal leadership changes occurred, and a collaborative culture emerged because distributed leadership requires strong collaboration across all levels in the system as well as across all content areas.

4. SUMMARY

An entire book could be written on how to create effective teacher teams or PLCs (e.g., DuFour et al., 2006) that result in multiple and distributed teacher and administrator leadership roles, a strong collaborative and professional school culture, and also higher levels of student performance. Collaborative and professional school cultures, today often called PLCs, are in the business of engaging teachers more in the key curriculum and decision-making processes of schools with the goal of making sure students are learning rather than just being taught; thus the prime focus of the PLCs or teacher data-based decision-making groups is on the linkages between student performance (formative, end of unit, benchmark, and summative) and the curriculum and instructional program. They are aggressive in seeking to improve student achievement by large, measurable amounts. They ground their work in data—both formative and summative data on student performance—and seek to link that data to improved instructional practice that also includes extra supports for students struggling to achieve up to high performance standards. Such professional and collaborative cultures also engage teachers in a much broader set of instructional leadership roles in the school, as well as the overall education system, thus helping also to create an education organization characterized by distributed leadership that includes teachers deploying a wide range of instructional leadership roles.

Professional and Best Practices

The ninth strategy is an element of the process of doubling student performance almost never explicitly mentioned in other studies, though it may be an implicit rather than an explicit message. The goal of this chapter is to raise this element of dramatically improving student performance in an explicit way. It concerns how the schools and districts did not draw on just their own knowledge, experience, and expertise but reached outside their system to the professional community. The schools and districts that doubled performance were highly professional in all their activities—reflecting what good professionals do; these organizations actively sought research evidence about how to improve schools, looked for best practices from other schools and districts, and identified and brought into their districts top experts who provided training on how teachers could deploy the best reading, mathematics, science, and writing practices in their classrooms.

No school or district that either my colleagues or I have studied produced such large improvements in student performance on their own. They reached out to the education community to find the most current and most appropriate curriculum, instruction, professional development, and change strategies that existed and tailored them for their schools. They read the research, they attended conferences, they listened to experts, they benchmarked best practices, and from that repository of professional knowledge they tailored a strategy for their school or district.

The first section describes various indicators of organizations acting in professional ways. Section 2 makes the point that truly professional organizations do not design change using only the knowledge of the people within them; that being professional means to reach out for knowledge, best practices, and top experts.

1. INDICATORS OF ACTING PROFESSIONALLY

No professional or professionally behaving organization tackles its problems only by tapping the knowledge of their own people. No authentically professional or professionally behaving organization would defer to its own philosophy or personal preference in addressing the complex problems it had to solve.

Seeking Research Knowledge

The essence of what it means to be a professional is knowing and deploying the core elements of what the profession has decided works. Doctors doing heart surgery or setting broken bones follow clear procedures; if they violate such procedures and a patient suffers, they can be sued for malpractice. To be sure, every specific surgery and bone repair has multiple unique aspects depending on the specific individual, the specific heart problem, or details of the broken bone. But there is a professional consensus about how to approach those procedures, and all doctors are expected to follow them as a matter of deploying sound professional practice; if they do not, they can be charged with unprofessional practice.

In too many instances, education comes up short in these sets of professional behaviors. Too often, teachers and principals have their "own philosophy" about how to engage in teaching or leading and explicitly reject research and best practices as "constraining" their creativity and approach to their work.

For example, I have had the experience of summarizing the research on best practices for educating gifted and talented students for principals and other school leaders; in large school districts, the best and least-cost strategy is to put such gifted students in separate classes and vastly accelerate instruction to let them learn two to three years of content in just one year. This strategy seems to violate deep-seated views about equity. So upon hearing this synthesis, many principals say some version of, "I don't care what the research says; that is not going to happen in my school."

By contrast, the teachers, principals, and other leaders in the doubling-performance sites actively and eagerly sought research evidence on the issues they were facing and referenced that research when discussing changes they made. They would reallocate resources to reduce class sizes to 15 in Grades K–3 because there was experimental, controlled research that found that such small class sizes were effective at those grades, and even more effective for low-income and minority students. They stressed phonics for very young children, citing research on the importance of phonemic awareness and the need to structure the teaching of phonics to many students from lower-income backgrounds. They knew about research on certain mathematics curriculum, like that of *Everyday Mathematics* (which is based on multiple years of research at the University of Chicago), and adopted that text series as a means to having students attain more problem-solving expertise in mathematics. Many schools and districts that put instructional coaches in schools as a key part of their overall professional development programs cited the research on professional development, showing that without coaching such training rarely has lasting impact and does not change classroom practice. And schools that extended learning time either through tutoring, extended-day programs, summer school, or double periods in secondary school cited research on the importance of extending learning time while holding standards for performance constant.

By noting the above, I am not arguing that the teachers, principals, and leaders in the double-performing schools always knew all the best research or interpreted all the research correctly or selected texts only with hard-core, research-based evidence. The point merely is that they actively sought the research on the issues they addressed and worked hard to incorporate it into their key decisions and their classroom practices.

Accessing Research

It should be noted, moreover, that accessing research on various issues facing most schools that need to double student performance is not that complex, contrary to many practitioners who claim that it is. Some claim that the reason many educators do not reference research as a source for action is because too few individuals in education seek out research evidence—that it is less the availability of good research, or summaries of it, and more the lack of will to seek it out. There may be some truth to that assertion, but I am not making that point. Yes, it does take effort to seek research evidence, but one does not need to be an academic to either find such evidence or to understand it; multiple channels are available to practitioners:

- *Education Week,* the nation's education newspaper, publishes articles on both emerging research findings as well as best practices across a range of issues.
- *Phi Delta Kappan* and *Educational Leadership,* the professional and practitioner-oriented journals that periodically have research syntheses written by leading researchers and practitioner-focused scholars—these syntheses are goldmines for busy practitioners.

- *American Educator,* a solidly research-based journal published by the American Federation of Teachers (AFT) provides excellent summaries and syntheses of best practices; excellent examples of such contributions include the Torgeson (2004) article on reading practices and the recent Goldenberg (2008) review of what works in teaching English-language learning (ELL) students and what more needs to be learned. The AFT also has been a supporter of the E. D. Hirsch approach to a classical curriculum and has published much in *American Educator* on the curriculum associated with that perspective.

Readers can also follow certain scholars who publish multiple articles on how to improve practice. For example, Bob Slavin writes prolifically on issues related to improving learning for children from disadvantaged backgrounds. These issues include student grouping, effective mathematics, and reading instruction (for the latter for example, see Slavin, Chamberlain, & Daniels, 2007) as well as comprehensive school designs.

In addition, all the major content associations in reading, science, mathematics, and so on publish not only research-focused journals but also practitioner-oriented journals, the former describing recent advances in teaching the content and the latter describing curriculum and classroom strategies for incorporating those instructional strategies into ongoing practice.

In short, practitioners can use numerous outlets to keep up with research knowledge about how to improve student learning in core subjects such as reading, writing, mathematics, and science. Given these multiple channels of information, there really is no excuse for not knowing about the most current advances in the field.

And as noted at the beginning of this chapter, the schools and districts that have produced large improvements in student academic achievement have many individuals who work to keep up with the most recent research knowledge—often using the above publications—and bring pertinent materials into the working teams of the system so that they can be systematically and professionally integrated into the strategies of that system. Indeed, Halverson's (2003) studies of how professional learning communities (PLCs) helped dramatically improve performance in a high-poverty, urban school references the key role played by the Breakfast Club, which was a group of teachers who met some morning every week to discuss a research article and its implications for their practice.

Seeking Best Practices

Another strategy deployed by districts and schools producing significant improvements in student learning is seeking out best practices. One example of this behavior in the past was attending "design fairs" organized by the various providers of comprehensive school designs. In a previous book on reallocating resources to fund school improvement, Odden and Archibald (2001a) identified several schools and districts that visited various design fairs as a key process in selecting a comprehensive approach to improving their school. Not only did these educational organizations participate in design fairs, but several also then visited schools that had implemented the designs in which they were interested. The seeking schools not only wanted to hear about the core features of new and more powerful school designs, which according to the designers were compilations of best practices in several areas, but also wanted to see how they were actually working in practice and to obtain the views of teachers and principals who were actually implementing them.

Other strategies include attending professional conferences or visiting other school systems; in both cases, the objectives are to hear about and/or see effective practices for the purpose of taking them home to use in one's own school or district.

Of course, teachers and principals do not always have to travel out of their districts or schools to find or view best practices. Indeed, getting all teachers to understand best instructional practices and use them in the classroom is the prime goal of most professional development and professional learning community activities, particularly those practices that have teachers observing other teachers expert at something instructional that needs to be learned, that have an instructional coach model an effective practice, and that have all teachers working in collaborative groups analyzing the instructional implications of formative assessments or the results of common end-of-unit student assessments. These are all within-school strategies for helping all teachers acquire and use best instructional practices in their own classroom, and they represent concrete ways schools can be organized to systematize best-practice-seeking behaviors.

Seeking Advice From Knowledgeable Others

The many examples of districts and schools producing large improvements in student learning that have been referenced in this book have included their reaching out both to consultants and other organizational entities whose mission it is to provide expert advice. Such consultants as Robert Marzano, who was once a top staff member of the Mid-Continent Regional Education Laboratory; Ruby Payne, an expert on educating children from poverty backgrounds; Marilyn Burns on teaching mathematical problem solving; JoEllen Killion at the National Staff Development Council, an expert on instructional coaches and professional development generally; and the DuFours on professional learning communities are just a few examples of high-quality consultants working around the country.

Nearly all schools and districts doubling student performance used one or more national consultant to help frame and implement their strategies.

Moreover, small rural districts like Abbotsford, Wisconsin, asked for assistance from their regional education service units and/or state departments of education. Abbotsford was a rural district not used to student diversity. All of a sudden it experienced fast growth in its population of students from Mexico, who were English language learners (ELL). The district sought assistance from both its regional service unit and the state education department, and in turn was provided knowledge and information and received training and even funding for the new and unique issues it faced with its new students whose primary language was not English. The assistance the school received helped it to improve reading achievement over several years even while the ELL population in the district was growing. The district did not struggle helplessly with how to be effective instructionally with ELL students—an area in which few in the district had previous knowledge or experience—nor did it ignore the issue and make no change, which likely would have produced falling performance. As good professionals, the administrators and teachers reached out to places where the professional knowledge they needed was supposed to reside, took in what those places provided, and improved their instructional program and impacts on students even as the district experienced growth in diversity it had never experienced before.

Abbotsford acted like a professional organization should.

2. NOT DOING IT ALONE

In this context, I am reminded of a school committed to improving performance in one urban district that was profiled in a national newspaper. This school faced severe and long-standing student performance issues and decided that the situation had to be changed. So the school committed to creating a new model for the school, what staff wanted to call the "Spaulding School" model[1] of education improvement. Their idea was that if faculty in this school could create a plan that worked, then other faculties would want to replicate their efforts.

The article lauded the school for this commitment; it was an example of an urban school that would no longer tolerate low levels of student achievement. And committing to broad-scale change was a first step in changing that school into one that was more effective.

On the other hand, the article gave no indication that this school was reaching out to the profession, research, or best practices as it was crafting the "Spaulding School" model. There was no hint that faculty and leadership in this school were reading the literature, interacting with experts, or learning about the best curriculum programs already out there.

The idea of the teachers and administrators was that they were going to design a new and more effective school by themselves. Given the wide array of professional information, knowledge, and examples of best practices that existed, the reporter should have asked the school people why they were not seeking that knowledge and why they felt they had to create everything from whole cloth: Why not build on the knowledge base that already existed? The newspaper article did not raise this critique, although it should have.

I would argue that not only was the idea of creating a new school design all alone actually unprofessional but also that it had very low chances of success. Why would one expect teachers and leaders who had worked for years in a low-performing school to suddenly have the expertise to improve the school, when they had tolerated low performance for so long? Further, even if the school *had* created a program that worked—that is, created the Spaulding School model—why would this faculty expect other faculties to pay any attention, since they hadn't paid attention to the broad and deep professional knowledge that already exists or to the scores and scores of effective schools programs all over the country? They had not looked at other programs that worked, so why would they assume that others would look at their new model?

The fact is that too many teachers and schools work in too much professional isolation and fall short of what they can do because they are unaware of the considerable professional knowledge of school transformation that already exists. The schools we studied that were successful in producing large gains in student learning and reducing the achievement gap in the process did not operate in isolation. They read as much research as possible, oftentimes in professional journals such as *Phi Delta Kappan* or *Educational Leadership,* or as synthesized in *Education Week,* reached out to experts to give them advice, tapped the expertise of formal groups created to provide technical assistance, searched for whole-school designs that had worked elsewhere in contexts like theirs, and created school structures designed to have all teachers searching for or creating best practices all the time in the normal course of their collaborative work in the school. In the process, they became what we would call professional organizations, deploying as best they could the state-of-the-art professional knowledge.

3. SUMMARY

So far, this book has identified nine important elements of the processes used in the schools that we and others have studied that produced dramatic improvements in student learning—what has been labeled as doubling performance. Schools in urban, suburban, and rural districts, schools with diverse and not-so-diverse populations, and both small and large schools around the country have been successful in producing quantum improvements in student achievement and in reducing achievement gaps. And the processes used by these schools and districts reflect the 10 strategies discussed in this book.

Although other authors (e.g., Blankstein, 2004; Chenoweth, 2007) might have a somewhat different set of key processes, the similarities across our findings and those of others is quite high. Even Grubb (2007), who studied how Finland dramatically improved student performance and also closed the achievement gap, found a very similar set of processes, though he also found that the Finns supported small classes, smaller secondary schools, and a more aggressive approach to teacher talent. At the same time, Grubb did not find that Finland simply spent money in order to gain higher achievements: Much was accomplished by recruiting into teaching only the best human capital and by reallocating existing resources and targeting new resources to paying teachers well, providing ample and ongoing professional development, and creating small schools and classrooms—strategies that also characterized the sites we studied that have doubled performance. The point here is that the ways to turn schools around and dramatically improve student performance are well known.

The challenge is to scale up these strategies to more schools and districts. As noted throughout this book, moreover, some of the processes for doubling student performance require considerable resources: extensive and ongoing professional development; reduced class sizes; and extended learning opportunities provided through tutoring, extended-day, and summer programs. Other elements of the process require only modest resources: analyzing state test data, setting high expectations, buying new curriculum materials (after they are worked into the regular instructional budget), getting and analyzing formative assessments, tapping the expertise of the profession, and creating a professional school culture. One strategy entailed using a fixed resource—time during the regular day—more effectively and thus more efficiently.

But a strategy that has received insufficient attention is that of the human capital needed to implement all of the above processes. Not any principal or any teacher is capable of engaging relentlessly in the process of doubling student performance; such talent needs to be recruited, developed, rewarded, and retained. The next chapter addresses these human capital issues, which are the foundation for how this country can dramatically improve student learning, particularly for students from low-income and minority backgrounds in urban and rural districts

NOTES

1. A pseudonym.

The Human Capital Side of Doubling Student Performance[1]

To improve student achievement, schools and districts need a powerful and ambitious "education improvement strategy." The previous chapters of this book have addressed several elements of such a strategy, elements that many, if not hundreds, of schools and districts across the country have used and in the process produced large improvements in student academic achievement—what the book calls a doubling of student performance over a time period of four to six years.

But each school and district also needed people to implement their education improvement strategies, and getting the talent needed is an important 10th strategy in the process of doubling performance. Few studies of school improvement, however, address the people, or what many call the talent and human-capital side of education improvement. But talent is important for all organizations seeking to dramatically improve performance. In the private sector, strategic talent management is an issue that is central for companies today that need to maintain competitive advantage and boost results (Lawler, 2008).

1. OVERVIEW[2]

Principal and teacher talent are key to improving student performance. And some districts, particularly those in urban and rural areas, face real talent problems—both shortages of numbers and insufficient quality. Indeed, research has documented the multiple problems with teacher and principal talent in large urban districts and their high-poverty, high-needs schools, problems that severely limit their abilities to improve instruction and student learning (for a summary, see Odden & Kelly, 2008). These problems include the following:

- The historic difficulty nationwide in attracting the "best and brightest" into teaching
- The difficulty many urban districts have in staffing high-need (high-poverty, low-achieving) schools with quality teachers and principals, which means schools open each fall with classrooms without full-time teachers or teachers not trained to teach
- Chronic shortages of qualified math, science, and technology teachers
- High teacher turnover, particularly in urban districts and the highest-need schools
- Professional development systems that spend upward of $6,000 to $8,000 per teacher per year, with little impact on instructional practice and very little focus on the core subjects of mathematics, science, reading, and writing
- Compensation systems that pay for factors not linked to student learning gains—years of experience and miscellaneous education units, no differentiation for areas experiencing teacher shortages, and few if any elements linked to the core goal of the system—student performance
- Lack of a talent acquisition, development, and management strategy

Over the past decade, however, leaders in several large, urban districts in the country, as well as some of the districts and schools that have doubled performance, concluded that they could not dramatically enhance student performance without top teacher and principal talent. They also concluded that if their districts were to make headway on their ambitious education reform and student performance goals, they needed to revamp the systems that recruited, deployed, inducted, developed, evaluated, paid, and managed their strategic human assets—high-quality teachers and school leaders.

A new national project that emerged in 2008 called the Strategic Management of Human Capital (SMHC) is addressing these talent and human capital management problems in the education system focusing first on the nation's largest and most urban districts. To guide this effort, Odden and Kelly (2008) developed a framework defining strategic management of human capital in education.

Two aspects of the strategic management of human capital are critical to dramatically improving the performance of America's school districts and were embedded in the strategies of the urban schools and districts doubling performance. The first is talent. These schools and districts figured out how to acquire top teacher and principal talent. These educational systems needed top talent at all levels, from teachers to top district leadership, to positions in the central office such as the human resource management systems, to leadership positions in schools, and to instructional leadership for every classroom and teaching context. And they developed successful strategies to acquire top talent. This chapter identifies the key elements of those strategies, drawing primarily on SMHC case studies of Boston (Archibald, 2008), Chicago (Kimball, 2008), and New York City (Goertz & Levin, 2008) but also on additional SMHC cases of Fairfax County (Milanowski, 2008), Long Beach (Koppich, 2008), and talent recruitment organizations such as Teach For America (Aportela & Goetz, 2008b), The New Teacher Project (Goetz & Aportela, 2008), and New Leaders for New Schools (Aportela & Goetz, 2008a).

A second issue is talent management. It was not sufficient for districts and schools just to find top talent and turn them loose. As the private sector has learned over the past decade, the highest-performance organizations not only recruit top talent but also manage and train them in ways that support the strategic directions of the organization. Several chapters of this book have already addressed how districts doubling student performance organized, managed, and trained teacher and principal talent; the training was part of an overall system of what SMHC would call "strategic" because many aspects of the human resource management systems in these education systems were aligned to their visions of effective instructional practice, including, at least to some degree, recruitment, screening, selection, placement, induction, professional development, and some aspects of instructional leadership.

To make talent management practices even more strategic, they need to be linked vertically to the educational improvement strategy and horizontally across all its key elements—recruitment, selection/placement, induction, mentoring, professional development, performance management/ evaluation, compensation, and instructional leadership—so that they produce the people with the knowledge and skills needed to execute the overall improvement strategy. Private sector companies applying a strategic approach to human resource management design those programs directly from their organizational improvement strategies (Boudreau & Ramstad, 2007; Gratton, Hope-Hailey, Stiles, & Truss, 1999; Lawler, 2008; Lawler, Boudreau, & Mohrman, 2006).

The remainder of this chapter discusses how several urban districts are beginning to remedy their teacher and principal talent shortages and have begun but have not yet fully aligned all their human capital management programs around their systems' views of effective instructional practice. It has three major sections, one addressing talent acquisition, one on talent development and retention, and one on the issue of turnover and reconstitution, an issue difficult to discuss in education.

2. FIRST, RECRUIT TOP TALENT

The talent acquisition strategies discussed below for Boston, Chicago, and New York are strategies from urban districts that have doubled student performance.

- Boston School District Stats
  - Employees: 5,000
  - Number of schools: 144
  - Students served: approximately 56,000
  - Student demographics
    - 41% African American
    - 35% Hispanic
    - 14% White
    - 9% Asian/Pacific Islander
    - 1% multiracial or American Indian
  - Performance gains from 1998 to 2004, Boston
    - Increased the percentage of students passing the 10th-grade math Massachusetts Comprehensive Assessment System (MCAS) on their first try from 25% to 74%
    - Increased similar results for the English MCAS from 43% to 77%

In addition, Boston won the Broad Prize for Urban Education in 2006—after four years as a finalist. This national award honors urban school districts that have demonstrated the greatest overall improvement in student achievement and progress toward the closing of the achievement gap (Archibald, 2008).

- Chicago School District Stats
  - The country's third largest school district
  - Employees: 40,000

- 25,000 teachers
- 600 principals
  - Number of schools
    - 480 elementary schools
    - 120 high schools
  - Student demographics
    - 48.6% African American
    - 37.6% Latino
    - 8.1% White
    - 5.7% other
    - Over 85% low income
    - Approx 14% limited English proficiency
  - Performance gains from 2001 to 2007, Chicago
    - Increased the percentage scoring proficient or advanced on the Illinois standards achievement test from 39% to 61% in reading and from 35% to 69% in mathematics (Kimball, 2008)
- New York City School District Stats
  - The largest school district in the United States
  - Number of teachers: approximately 79,000
  - Number of schools: 1,450
  - Number of students: 1,040,000
  - Student demographics
    - 32% African American
    - 39% Hispanic
    - 14% White
    - 14% Asian/Pacific Islander
    - 14% enrolled as English language learners (ELL)
    - Nearly 19% receive special education services
  - Performance gains from 2002 to 2008, New York
    - The percentage of students scoring at or above proficient on the state mathematics test rose 28 percentage points (to 80%) in the fourth grade and 30 percentage points (to 60%) in eighth grade.
    - The percentage of students scoring at or above proficient on the state reading assessment rose from 46% to 61% in the fourth grade and from 30% to 43% in the eighth grade (Goertz & Levin, 2008).

In sum, all three districts produced impressive student learning gains, doubling performance in many cases and tripling performance in one case. A key part of their strategy was to enhance the talent pool of teachers and administrators. The discussion that follows draws largely on the talent strategies of these districts but also integrates the people issues of the schools and districts that have doubled performance discussed previously in this book.

Acquiring Talent

In a cross-case analysis of the various strategies Boston, Chicago, New York, and other SMHC case studies districts used to find top teacher and principal talent, Koppich and Showalter (2008) concluded that urban districts indeed can recruit top-quality teachers and principals. They can do so by deploying a set of aggressive, well-designed, comprehensive, and multifaceted recruitment strategies.

Koppich and Showalter as well as many others (Levin & Quinn, 2003) concluded that the teacher shortages, lack of adequate talent, and school staffing vacancies typical of so many urban districts and their high-need schools need not be part of the "DNA" of urban school systems; these shortcomings largely resulted from a lack of attention to recruiting. Too many districts, including the districts studied, had left "recruitment" to late August. By this time, the individuals who had applied earlier to the district, but were ignored, had already taken jobs in other districts. Indeed, Washington, D.C., typically had 2,500 applicants each year, with only 250 vacancies, a ratio of 10 applicants for every position. But before Michelle Rhee became chancellor in summer of 2007, the district had ignored those applicants, which included significant numbers of talented and well-trained teachers, many with math and science majors. By late August when the district began to act, most good applicants were no longer available, and the district, like Boston, Chicago, and New York City a decade earlier, opened school with scores of classrooms filled with unqualified teachers—and some classrooms without even unqualified teachers.

Actively Recruit Teachers and Principals

The SMHC districts remedied these teacher shortcomings with comprehensive recruitment strategies. Active recruitment can identify top talent who will apply and accept job offers in urban districts. Chicago, for example, rather than take teachers from just the lowest-ranked colleges and teacher-training programs close to the city, the pattern of the past, began to recruit in top colleges with excellent teacher-training programs close to the district, such as Northwestern University, the University of Illinois at Champaign-Urbana, the University of Chicago, the University of Wisconsin–Madison, and the University of Michigan. To their pleasant surprise, many young prospective teachers from these top universities were eager to teach in the city and most became effective teachers. Further, district human resource leaders read the research that most teachers hold jobs in school districts within 50 miles of where they grew up or went to college. Interpreting this as a desire to stay "close to home," Chicago began recruiting at top teacher-training universities within a 500-mile radius of Chicago, arguing that if they taught in Chicago they would be only a "one day's drive back home." And the district found many additional new teachers from the University of Kansas, Kansas State University, the University of Iowa, Vanderbilt, and so on who also were more than willing to teach in the district's high-need schools. New York City works with local universities to promote teaching among undergraduate and graduate students. The district provides tuition reimbursement at the City University of New York rate for teachers certified in nonshortage areas who are willing to become certified in shortage areas.

So one talent recruitment strategy was to strengthen relations with and recruit from high-quality, traditional teacher-training colleges and universities.

Tap Nontraditional Sources and National Organizations for Top Talent

A second strategy was to recruit through "alternative" certification routes by partnering with national talent recruiting organizations such as The New Teacher Project (TNTP) (Goetz & Aportela, 2008), Teach For America (TFA) (Aportela & Goetz, 2008b), Troops to Teachers and, for principals, New Leaders for New Schools (Aportela & Goetz, 2008a). TFA receives thousands of applications each year from graduates of the country's top colleges and universities; in some years, up to 10% of the graduating classes of Harvard, Brown, Princeton, Duke, Northwestern, and other top universities apply to TFA for at least a two-year stint in a high-poverty school; 44% generally stay beyond that minimum time commitment. TNTP also has thousands of applicants from early- and midcareer changers from the financial industry (with even more thousands out of work in 2008 and 2009 due to the collapse of the financial system), law firms, management consulting companies, and other high-demand jobs in the private sector; most are willing to take a huge salary cut to do meaningful work as a teacher in a high-need school. Scores of such individuals bring strong math, science, and statistics majors with them, just the type of content knowledge in short supply in urban districts.

Indeed, Arne Duncan, whom President Barack Obama chose as his first Secretary of Education, set a goal to acquire 20% of all new Chicago teachers from alternative-route sources. In public comments, he has said that it would have been a disservice to the district to depend only on individuals who at the age of 18 decided to enter teacher training as a college undergraduate. All alternative-route providers recruit and train individuals *after* they have received their bachelor's degree and sometimes after working in the private sector for four to seven years. Thus, districts need strong induction, mentoring, professional development, and evaluation systems to ensure that such teachers acquire the kind of instructional expertise needed to be effective in the urban context.

Grow Your Own Teachers and Principals

Third, all three districts—Boston, Chicago, and New York City—created "grow your own" teacher and principal programs. These programs provided training targeted to the specific needs of these districts and their visions of effective instruction, but they also engaged both teachers and principals in a year of "residency" during which they taught under the supervision of a mentor while they acquired sufficient expertise to be a full-fledged teacher or principal. In some cases, such as those in Chicago, these urban resident programs were run in concert with a local university, but in other cases, such as those in Boston, the district ran the program with its own staff (though often "stealing" its instructors from local colleges of education, which as institutions were not willing to work closely with the district).

Use an Array of Incentives

Fourth, the districts provided incentives to enhance recruitment efforts. For example, New York City eliminated all "emergency certified" teachers and initiated the Housing Support Program that offers approximately $15,000 to experienced math, science, and special-education teachers who are employed outside New York City and who agree to teach for at least three years in one of the district's high-needs schools. Teachers of Tomorrow, a New York State initiative, offers newly hired teachers the chance to earn a tax-free grant of $3,400 for each year of satisfactory service up to four years for teaching in a high-needs school. The district also increased teacher salaries by 43% from 2003 to 2008.

Recruiting Works

What the districts discovered was that "if you recruit, they will come." They found that there were hundreds, and thousands nationally, of highly talented individuals from many sources who would be willing to teach in an urban school if they were actually recruited and a pathway was created for their entry into the system. Today, these school systems have more than 10 applicants for each open teacher position, subject all applicants to a rigorous review and interview process, and open school each fall with no teacher and principal vacancies in core subjects. External studies have shown that by any measure, the quality of their teacher and principal corps has dramatically improved, as has student achievement. Indeed, the superintendents in these districts say they have the most talented teachers and administrators their schools have ever experienced.

New Policies and Practices to Facilitate New Recruitment Initiatives

The districts also created several new policies, and through negotiations with their unions changed many traditional policies to support these new recruitment strategies:

1. They devolved a selection of teachers to school sites. Central offices could no longer place any teachers in schools unilaterally, nor could senior teachers move into the school on the basis of seniority.

2. Only teachers selected by the principal, usually with advice provided by a team of teachers, were employed at the school.

3. Districts moved up the budget calendar, so schools knew their school budget—and thus the number of teachers they needed to hire—by the end of winter—around late February or early March.

4. Senior teachers were the first people allowed to apply for vacancies, so they had the first shot at an open job, but they got the job only if selected by the school. This procedure usually required substantial change in the contract language for teacher transfers across schools.

5. All districts "automated" their recruitment and screening systems so that all jobs were posted online, teachers applied online, initial screening was done electronically, and all applicants received feedback on their applications within a few days of the filing the initial application. Further, special candidates—such as those with math and science majors, minority candidates, and males at the elementary level—received early job offers, perhaps not knowing then in which school they would work but knowing the district would provide them a teaching job for the upcoming school year.

6. When hired, the teachers were immediately put on payroll and signed up for benefits, because the districts' recruitment software was linked to its salary and benefits software. As a result, the districts solved yet another problem they had faced historically— they paid teachers correctly and at the end of the first month on the job, rather than late and incorrectly.

In sum, through a series of recruitment initiatives, some but not all described above, as well as multiple changes in policies and practices, these districts were able to recruit and place large numbers of talented teachers and principals in high-need schools, thus providing the talent needed to implement their overall education improvement strategies. And the overall set of efforts worked: Teacher and principal quality rose as did student learning. The districts are not fully satisfied, however, with their efforts, and while proud of the accomplishments they have made, they know that much more progress needs to be made—that even though they have doubled student performance in many areas, student learning still needs to improve to higher levels, especially in those subjects and grades that have not yet experienced the doubling of performance.

3. SECOND, DEVELOP TOP TALENT

Because teacher and principal quality were such prime challenges for urban districts, the districts that were the subject of SMHC cases addressed the recruitment issues most aggressively and comprehensively. Koppich and Showalter (2008) concluded that while the districts studied were addressing the issues of talent development and management, few had managed to align all key human resource programs and practices around the instructional vision of the district. Districts had strengthened new teacher induction, enhanced professional development sometimes but not always tightly linked to a rigorous curriculum and the systems' view of effective instructional practices, created their own programs for training principals beyond requiring individuals to be state certified, experimented with new approaches to evaluation for both teachers and principals, and created a few compensation innovations. However, in no case were *all* of these new initiatives anchored in the core set of instructional competencies teachers and principals need to boost student learning.

Boston (Archibald, 2008) and Long Beach (Koppich, 2008) made the most progress in linking together key human resource programs around the districts' core vision of effective instructional practice. By partnering with its prime university provider of teachers—California State University at Long Beach—Long Beach first aligned university teacher training with its core instructional vision. And the district's new teacher induction, mentoring and professional developments all were aligned with the Essential Elements of Teaching, which defined how the district approached instructional practice.

Boston accomplished these linkages by partnering with the Boston Plan for Excellence, which is a local education foundation that works in close partnership with Boston to refine professional development for teachers and principals and improve instruction in classrooms. And since they were unsuccessful in inducing local universities to align how they trained teachers with Boston's view of good instruction, the district created its own new teacher-training program, called the Boston Teacher Residency Program.

However, neither Boston nor Long Beach, nor the other urban districts studied by SMHC, strongly linked either teacher or principal evaluation to the system's view of good teaching, though all districts aspire to make such connections in the future.

These alignment aspirations reflect how instructional practice should be central to district and school operations, much like the districts and schools doubling performance that have been profiled in the preceding chapters of this book. These effective schools and districts have linked all their key actions—high goals for student learning, data-based decision making, professional development, collaborative work on the instructional program, formal and informal teacher evaluation, and so on—to the vision of effective instruction that is at the center of their work. Though all these schools and districts would admit that further progress and stronger linkages could be made, their intent is to anchor the major human resources programs (recruiting, induction, mentoring, professional development, evaluation and pay) in the skills and competencies teachers need to make their instructional practice more powerful so as to boost student learning to much higher levels I would expect that if their evaluation and compensation systems also were more tightly connected to their vision of effective instructional practice, their efforts to improve classrooms and boost student learning would be even more effective (Odden, 2008).

4. SOMETIMES INITIAL TALENT TURNOVER IS REQUIRED

Although the issue of teacher and principal talent did not emerge as a "problem" in all the schools and districts that have doubled performance, the fact is that the issue of good talent is more central in some places than most case studies have reported.

Some urban districts, it should be noted, moreover, have concluded that recruiting top talent to fill natural vacancies due to retirement and other movements of teachers does not represent all aspects of the first step of talent acquisition. In some urban districts around the country, district leaders have concluded that more dramatic changes in talent are needed, sometimes at both the district office and in many schools. For example, Anthony Alvarado reduced the central office in both New York City

District 2 and San Diego by literally scores of individuals as part of his widely admired educational improvement strategy; in those cases, the saved resources were turned into professional development—training and school-based instructional coaches—provided to all teachers. Joel Klein in New York City and Michelle Rhee in Washington, D.C., also dramatically cut jobs in the central office as well as in schools, sending the saved funds back to the schools.

Alvarado's success in boosting student learning, particularly through improved reading instruction, in New York City's District 2 is widely acclaimed by teachers, union leaders, administrators, and scholars (see Elmore & Burney, 1999). But one aspect of that success that has rarely been discussed was that over the four- to six-year time period during which the district implemented his reforms, he replaced two-thirds of the principals and 50% of the teachers as the district implemented its educational improvement plan that focused on a specific view of reading instruction. The district retained only those teachers who agreed to and did teach that instructional approach in their reading classrooms and only principals who could see whether such instructional practices were being used and could help teachers improve the specific instructional practice. In short, a large turnover of teachers and principals was part of the overall improvement process.

Likewise, school reconstitution across the country is characterized by replacing all the individuals in historically low-performing schools, and many examples of schools and districts dramatically improving performance have this significant change in talent element (see Chenoweth, 2007). For example, one notable large-scale effort that doubled student performance is the Benwood Initiative that was implemented in Hamilton County, Tennessee, which is the home of Chattanooga (see Silva, 2008). After the city merged with the county school system, it became widely known that performance in the city schools, which had higher concentrations of children from low-income and minority backgrounds, was much lower than in the more suburban county schools. Teacher and principal talent was also far below that in the suburban part of the district. The merged district decided that these conditions were not acceptable.

So with help from the local Benwood Foundation, it launched a large-scale change effort that mirrors quite strongly the 10 strategies in this book. According to Silva (2008), the initiative included setting ambitiously high expectations for student learning, focusing initially on literacy, using formative assessments with a team-based approach to analyzing such data, providing intensive and ongoing professional development, including the placement of reading coaches in all schools, anchoring all professional development in the district view of good reading instructional practice, providing extra help to struggling students, replacing principals in all the Benwood focus schools, creating a collaborative school culture, and providing incentives to individual teachers whose students showed large gains in performance as measured by the Tennessee-state summative tests. These strategies are quite aligned with those described in the previous chapters of this book. Further, it was the latter program element that has received some of the most attention in national accounts of this successful change initiative.

But another important element of the overall change was its approach to teacher and principal talent. All Benwood schools were "reconstituted"—that is, all principals and teachers were released. New principals were then placed in all the schools. While those new principals rehired nearly half of the original teaching faculty, substantial numbers were not rehired, and those who were rehired were rehired only if the school thought they had the basic talent to be successful and if they also committed to the overall instructional directions of the reconstituted school.

In short, the Benwood schools implemented a brand-new educational improvement strategy, with nearly the same 10 core strategies discussed in this book. But the point of this example is to note that there was also a "people" or talent side to the reform initiative. Because the district had concluded that many of the teachers in the city schools were not that effective, in contrast to the vast bulk of staff in the suburban schools of the merged district, district leaders decided that a large change in teachers (and principals) was needed as an integral part of the overall reform strategy. Thus, before trying to implement a new educational improvement strategy, the district changed the bulk of the people at the schools. And after receiving a new principal and deciding which teachers to hire back, each school then launched a recruitment process to fill all remaining teaching vacancies. These people changes were activated in order for the schools to have the principal and teacher talent required to implement the ambitious set of strategies designed to dramatically improve student performance.

5. SUMMARY

As this chapter has argued, it takes talent to implement educational strategies designed to dramatically improve—if not double—student academic learning. And although the people side of these powerful improvement strategies has not been that central a part of cases of school improvement in the past, teacher and principal talent are nevertheless a core and critical part of being able to effectively implement powerful education improvement strategies.

This chapter has also shown that shortages of top teachers and principals are something that should not be accepted and can be remedied in urban school districts. When districts do little recruiting and begin the personnel selection process at the end of the summer, they miss out on acquiring the talent they need. But several urban districts, including Boston, Chicago, and New York City, have shown that with comprehensive and multipronged recruitment strategies urban districts can find and hire top teacher and principal talent.

Moreover, as the successful Benwood Initiative in Chattanooga showed, sometimes a substantial change in staff is an integral part of successful school reform. Though school reconstitution is unpopular in many education circles, a history of placing large numbers of unqualified teachers in high-need schools might not be fully remedied by professional development, and many districts, like that of Hamilton County, conclude that change in school leadership along with considerable change in the school's faculty might have to be part of a successful school transformation.

The bottom line is that a critical part of effective education improvement is the quality of leadership and teaching talent in each school. Every school needs to give attention to the quality of that talent pool and take efforts to ensure that it has a sufficient supply of top teacher and principal talent that it both needs and deserves.

NOTES

1. The research on most of the schools and districts doubling performance did not focus much on their acquisition of talented teachers and principals, thus there is much less information from those studies on this issue. On the other hand, a prime focus of the studies of Boston, Chicago, and New York was on their approaches to finding top teacher and principal talent, and thus most of the specific details in this chapter on talent acquisition derive from those cases. The general findings, however, could apply to any district that had shortages of qualified teachers and principals. Unfortunately, the chapter was not able to address the specifics of how rural districts can find talent, and that is an issue that needs more analytic attention.

2. The remainder of this chapter draws heavily from Koppich and Showalter (2008).

Putting It All Together

The Dramatically Improving School

This chapter provides a compilation of all the elements in the preceding chapters that characterize a dramatically improving school. This synthesis of the dramatically improving school also reflects my experience of what leading educators from across the country have told me about what it takes to produce large improvements in student learning; indeed, these were also the core conclusions of a group of leading educators in Wyoming convened in late 2008 by Picus and Associates. Each of the following subsections succinctly describes one of the aspects of the improving school. Although the synthesis is provided in a chronological order, it is also the case that for most schools and districts their efforts are not always implemented in a linear order; rather, each element is developed and refined as needed.[1]

1. THE CORE ELEMENTS OF THE IMPROVING SCHOOL

The sections below summarize what is written in the previous 10 chapters. This chapter ends with a distillation of the overall process provided by leaders in the Kennewick School District in Washington State.

Understanding the Performance Situation

The dramatically improving school begins its process of improvement by understanding that it has a performance problem and that current levels of performance are far from desired levels. Faculty use state summative student achievement data and in many cases also draw from additional student achievement data from such sources as the NWEA MAP (Northwest Evaluation Association Measures of Academic Performance) system. The school analyzes these data to determine in what areas its students are performing well and in what areas performance needs to improve. These data also help school leaders and teachers identify the nature and existence of achievement gaps that may exist in the school. The state data analyses provide a "macro" map of performance strengths and weaknesses of the school. Depending on the scope and breadth of the state testing data, these initial analyses also provide some information on subissues, such as performance on various state content standards. Additional information on student performance, such as benchmark data from the NWEA MAP system, provide even more detail on performance by subtopics and concepts included in the district's and state's curriculum standards.

Curriculum Mapping

Along with the analysis of such data, the dramatically improving school, together with the school district, creates a "curriculum map" or "curriculum scope" designed to take the state's curriculum content standards and identify the topics and subtopics that must be taught, subject by subject and grade by grade, in order to cover all material in the state standards. The goal of this mapping exercise is both to identify any gaps in the district's content standards, and, going forward, to identify the content that should be taught to all students so that they are fully prepared to take the state summative tests at the end of the year, with such state tests theoretically assessing student performance in the curriculum the state wants all students to learn.

One might expect that this process would produce similar curriculum maps and scopes across subjects, grades, schools, and districts, because the results derive from the same state curriculum standards. This may not always happen, however, because the specificity of each state's curriculum standards allows some local flexibility in content to be taught and because state tests might not be a perfectly aligned measure of student achievement to the state standards.

Nevertheless, the goal of this curriculum-mapping exercise at the district and school level is to identify a curriculum scope and sequence of subtopics for each content area and each grade level that is intended to represent the core content to be taught to all students. Further, many districts and schools add "pacing" schedules to this curriculum scope and sequence, providing the time periods over which certain curriculum content should be taught during the course of the school year. One goal of the pacing schedules is to ensure that students are taught the core content included in the state curriculum standards with student learning measured by state tests.

Set High Goals

Using the state tests as the anchor, and sometimes benchmark student achievement data as well, the dramatically improving school sets high goals for student achievement. One common goal is for all, or nearly all, students to achieve at least to the proficiency level of the state summative tests, including most state end-of-course high school tests. In other cases, schools and districts set a goal to reduce any achievement gaps, such as those that might exist for at-risk students, students with a learning disability, students with minority or Native American backgrounds, or students who come from homes where English is not the primary language. The dramatically improving school wants to move from being a "good" (or even not so good) school to being a "great" school.

The goals identify targets for student performance that require large, absolute gains in student achievement that usually go beyond just meeting AYP (Adequate Yearly Progress) under the federal No Child Left Behind program. The dramatically improving school does want to make AYP, but over time it also wants its students to make more than marginal increases in performance; it wants the vast bulk—95%—of students to achieve at or above proficiency. And it wants that achievement to be "authentic," or representative of real learning. Further, the dramatically improving school wants to produce this high level of learning for all students, including the increasing numbers of students from poverty, minority, and non-English-speaking backgrounds.

Many times, these goals are expressed as a desire to be among the "best" schools in the state or the "best" urban district in the country. As written in Chapter 2, the goals might seem outlandish, and they certainly are bold and go far beyond marginal improvements, but they reflect the long-standing American value of thinking big, taking risk, working hard, and attaining what many might think is impossible.

Adopt New Curriculum Materials and Create a Point of View About Instruction

One way the dramatically improving school strives to meet its goals is by adopting new, and what the school feels are research-based, curriculum programs. A popular elementary math curriculum is *Everyday Mathematics,* which stresses both basic and problem-solving skills. There is more variation in the reading texts selected and some districts and schools also create their own reading curriculum, but the reading curriculum is almost always a "balanced" reading program, with emphases on phonemic awareness and phonics for very young learners, vocabulary, reading fluency, reading comprehension, and writing. But nearly every school and district adopts or creates new curriculum materials, concluding that their previous curriculum materials were the foundation of their previous performance situation and not appropriate for attaining their bold, new achievement goals.

Over time, the dramatically improving school develops a clear point of view about good instructional practice, although the specifics can vary by district. Improving schools have created a number of approaches to good instruction such as:

- A balanced reading program as a point of view about effective reading instruction
- Essential elements of instruction
- A clear goal and purpose for a lesson plan and acquiring student work that can be scored on the basis of performance rubrics to determine if the goal/purpose was met
- Four aspects of good instruction, including classroom management, curriculum planning, instruction, and assessment
- "Brain-based" instruction, which has a variety of interpretations
- The instructional strategies advocated by consultant Marzano

Regardless of the approach taken to identify and implement good instructional practice, the dramatically improving school has clear and specific notions of what effective instructional practice looks like, and over time it expects all teachers to acquire and use those instructional practices in their classrooms.

To facilitate growth in student achievement at the dramatically improving school, the curriculum materials and point of view of effective instructional practice are common across all the schools in the district. This represents a change in practice from several years ago when curriculum, textbooks, and instructional practice often varied not only across schools within a district but also across classrooms within individual schools and sometimes even among classrooms at the same grade level or focused on the same subject. The dramatically improving school recognizes that this kind of curriculum and instructional variability or inconsistency in instructional practice was not effective in producing large systemwide gains in achievement for all students. Rather, a more systemic curriculum and instructional approach is needed if the system as a whole, and each school in that system, is to be successful in educating more students to higher student performance standards.

Though the dramatically improving school uses specific curriculum materials and instructional programs, it does not view the programs themselves as the answer to high levels of student achievement. It believes that good instruction in reading, mathematics, or any subject entails certain fundamental tenets of what constitutes good instructional practice. And that is what the school focuses on systemically. As mentioned earlier, the dramatically improving school has concluded that a bundle of different programs focused on individual students has produced average performance in the past and as a strategy will not help a school move from good to great. To achieve greatness, the school recognizes that it needs an essential curriculum, an essential core set of instructional practices, and essential common assessments, used by all teachers and reinforced in multiple ways.

Instructional practice in the dramatically improving school is public and systemic and not private and individualistic. Professionalism in the school is viewed as engaging in collaborative work, often through professional learning communities (PLCs), on all aspects of the curriculum and instructional program, including assessment of the effectiveness of each individual teacher to a common set of both teaching standards and student performance assessments.

In the dramatically improving school, consistency of curriculum implementation and instructional practice is monitored by formal and informal "walk-throughs" by combinations of central-office staff, the principal, and instructional coaches. These individuals observe instructional practice and conduct post-walk-through conferences, focusing on their observations and comparing them to their expectations of curriculum and instructional practice. The dramatically improving school also relies on teachers to observe their peers. The dramatically improving school uses peer observations to press for "fidelity" in the implementation of the curriculum and the instructional program, believing that professionalism is reflected through consistent practice by all teachers and not idiosyncratic practice that varies across classrooms.

Data-Based Decision Making

The dramatically improving school relies on teams of teachers (grade-level teams in elementary schools and content teams in secondary schools) to collaboratively develop curriculum units that have common diagnostic/ formative assessments, comprehensive lesson plans, ongoing formal and informal formative assessments that can be used when teaching the various lesson plans, and common end-of-unit assessments. In addition to state test data and benchmark test data, such as NWEA MAP assessments, many schools also use DIBELS (Dynamic Indicators of Basic Early Literacy Skills), the Wireless Generation, and other more microformative assessment data for improving instruction. Teacher teams and PLCs work to analyze the results from the formative assessments, and often, with the help of instructional coaches, change instructional practice so as to tailor their teaching to the precise situation of their students.

Teacher teams in PLCs also use such formative assessments as they create/hone standards-based curriculum units, teach them with the support of instructional coaches, and collaboratively reflect on the success of the unit: Did students learn the goals and concepts of the unit, were the extra-help strategies for the struggling students successful, did their revised instructional strategies based on the formative assessment results work, and did student performance vary significantly by classroom and teacher?

This collaborative reflective assessment helps identify shortcomings of the unit, an assessment that was finalized on the basis of both formative assessment information as well as other professional knowledge about how students learn the concept covered by the unit, which the team can then improve for future classes. It also is used to identify how successful individual teachers are in their instructional practice and enables the instructional coaches to target their assistance to those teachers in the short term. Through the use of common end-of-unit assessments, teacher teams are able to engage in analyses of the impact of curriculum planning and instructional implementation.

Professional Development

The dramatically improving school provides intensive and ongoing professional development for all teachers to help them implement the common curriculum and instructional vision. Involvement in professional development is not voluntary; instead it is understood that changes in curriculum and instructional practice require all teachers to acquire new knowledge and expertise. Professional development is aided by district and school instructional coaches, who support the work of all teachers—some more intensively than others, depending on their experience and an assessment of their current practice. The goal is to help them implement effective instructional practices in their classrooms through observation and feedback. Instructional coaches model the best ways to deliver instruction and facilitate discussion about best and successful practices among teachers.

Teachers in the dramatically improving school do not create their "own" individual professional development plans. All teachers work mainly in collaborative teams, analyzing formative and end-of-unit assessments, discussing what is known about teaching various content concepts, and merging lesson plans that constitute a standards-based curriculum unit. Much of this collaborative work is done during "planning and preparation" periods, when all teachers in the team are scheduled so that their students are in elective classes and the teachers can meet and collaborate over various aspects of the curriculum and instructional program.

In most cases, teachers in the dramatically improving school have summer institutes where they receive intensive training, often in core content needed for various subjects, and then work with instructional coaches and collaborative teams to put that training into their practice over the course of the subsequent school year.

Use Time Effectively

The dramatically improving school uses time during the school day in different and, what for them became, more effective ways. The schools and districts did not extend the school day or year. They used a "fixed" resource—the six hours of instruction during the regular school day—in new and creative ways by increasing the minutes of instructional time for core subjects such as reading and mathematics, protecting core instructional time from outside interruptions, providing "double" periods for core subjects for students struggling to learn to proficiency, giving one-to-one and very small group tutoring extra help instead of elective classes, and employing other ways to maximize academic learning time (ALT) for core subjects for all students. By implementing a variety of essentially no-cost time-use strategies, schools used a resource more efficiently as the fixed resource now was used to produce a higher level of student achievement outcomes. The examples show that schools and districts, even being educational organizations, can think of doing business in more efficient ways.

Unfortunately, I did not find any examples of schools that reduced seven- or eight-period days back to six-period days, thus reducing costs and increasing instructional time in core subjects, but this should be a strategy schools consider in the future.

Schools also devised a variety of different and often ingenious ways to increase collaborative planning and instructional work time for teachers, oftentimes creating 90–120 minute blocks of time for this work at least once or twice during the typical school week.

Interventions for Struggling Students

The dramatically improving school knows that even the highest-quality core instruction provided to all students will not be sufficient for all students and that some students will struggle to achieve to higher standards. Thus, the dramatically improving school is also characterized generally by an "inclusion" approach to students with learning disabilities, by a "response to intervention" approach to any student struggling to achieve to a proficiency level, and by a tiered "continuum of extra services" and "differentiated instruction." This means that all students with disabilities, except those with the most severe and profound disabilities, are first taught the core content in the regular classroom, with the expectation over time that they achieve at least to the proficiency level of student performance. To achieve this goal, all students first experience high-quality instruction in the regular curriculum provided by the regular classroom teacher. If a student has a mild struggle, the regular teacher offers some within-class extra help, such as a small group that receives extra instruction a few times during the week, a calculator for a student with calculation challenges, helping disorganized secondary students simply organize their notebooks, or other similar "modest extra-effort, extra-help" strategies.

The next tier of intervention is more intensive. It might be provided within the regular classroom or in a pull-out setting. This tier of intervention includes some combination of individual or small-group (three to five students) tutoring provided by a licensed teacher. In some cases, this tutoring is provided by a trained and supervised instructional aide. Trained aides, however, do not tutor the students with the most complex learning challenges, such as those in the bottom quartile—that is left to the expertise of a licensed, and sometimes specially trained, teacher. The second tier of intervention might also include an additional teacher working side by side with the regular teacher in the regular classroom to provide a series of continuous extra help for students who need that assistance.

The dramatically improving school also provides additional instructional help to students through some combination of "extended-day" (after school, before school, Saturday school) and/or summer school for students who, after receiving the aforementioned extra services within the regular school day, still need extra help to learn to a proficiency level. The exact combination of extended-day and summer school services, as well as the structure of these services, varies, but the dramatically improving school has or finds at least some resources to provide this level of additional help to some students.

If all of the previously identified extra-help strategies prove to be insufficient for the student to achieve proficiency, the dramatically improving school goes through the identification process and develops a formal individual education program (IEP) that specifies additional services to be provided under the state and federal special-education system.

Leadership and Professional Culture

Leadership in the dramatically improving school is "dense," meaning that leadership is provided by all levels of the system and by all actors in the system. The district is led by a superintendent who defines the mission of the district as teaching all students at least to the proficiency levels of the state test and also by curriculum experts who work with schools and teachers to develop a common curriculum scope and sequence that is aligned with the state standards and state testing system. Instructional coaches provide considerable instructional leadership as do principals.

Schools are characterized by a series of teacher teams—grade-level teams in elementary schools and subject-area teams in secondary schools—with each team having a teacher leader or coordinator. Some elementary schools also have cross-grade curriculum teams in core subjects such as math, reading, science, and history. The dramatically improving school might also have a curriculum council composed of all teacher team leaders, which provides oversight of the curriculum and instructional program and which is assisted by instructional coaches.

Today these teams are called PLCs. To facilitate the ongoing work of PLCs, the dramatically improving school is structured so that teachers in the various teams or PLCs have common planning periods during the school day, enabling them to meet together and work collaboratively on team business. The dramatically improving school is characterized in a variety of ways:

- A collaborative culture, which helps create and sustain high expectations for student learning
- Implementation of a common curriculum and instructional approach focused on producing consistent increases in student performance
- All staff taking responsibility for student achievement results—proud when performance rises and professional (asking how they can improve their own instructional practice to achieve better results) when performance does not rise

The culture in a dramatically improving school believes that improved student performance derives from improved instructional practice so that if student performance does not rise then something about instructional practice needs to be fixed.

A Professional Organization

The dramatically improving school is professional in the best sense of the term. Its teachers, instructional facilitators, and principals do not rely only on their own knowledge to improve student performance. Rather, they are aware of and read research on what works. They identify best practices from professional organizations. They bring the best consultants into their school to provide advice and training—Robert Marzano, Lucy Calkins, Ruby Payne, Harry Wong, Phil Schlecty, and others. They work with regional education units (e.g., the Mid-Continent Region Educational Laboratory) and with the State Department of Education. Their goal is to acquire the most current information on best practices and what works and to incorporate that knowledge into their overall school program.

The dramatically improving school also tracks the impact of all its key initiatives, continuing those programs that work (produce the desired student achievement results) and dropping those that do not.

Address Talent and Human Capital Issues

The dramatically improving school knows that talented teachers and principals matter—a lot. They seek to hire the best teachers and administrators, induct them into their professional cultures, equip them with the instructional strategies needed to be successful in their new schools, supervise and evaluate them to rigorous professional standards, and pay them a good wage.

Schools in dramatically improving urban districts play major roles in new teacher and principal recruitment strategies. They are very pleased that the district has initiated broad and comprehensive teacher recruitment strategies; they are able to review the applicants of multiple and qualified candidates for nearly all positions, have interviews with those in whom they are most interested, and make the final selections. Seniority bumping is no longer allowed, though senior teachers have priority in applying for any new positions.

2. SUMMARY

The dramatically improving school's approach to curriculum, instruction, and professional development is characterized by the following:

- High expectations for the learning of all students, expectations that exceed AYP
- A common school and districtwide curriculum that is taught in all subjects and all grade levels
- A common instructional approach that is viewed by the district and school as the most effective for this educational system
- Significant ongoing data-based analyses using diagnostic, formative, and common end-of-curriculum-unit tests
- Curriculum units collaboratively shaped by teacher teams, taught simultaneously, and then assessed for impact
- Intensive, ongoing professional development with heavy involvement and engagement of instructional coaches in all aspects of professional development and the implementation of the curriculum and instructional program
- Creation of a collaborative school culture with multiple PLCs
- Distributed instructional leadership provided by both site teachers and administrators, reinforced by supportive and facilitative actions by central-office staff

In the dramatically improving school instruction is key—there is the strongly held belief that improved student achievement results from improved instructional practice linked to a rigorous, content-rich curriculum program. Absent improved instruction and good curriculum, student learning is unlikely to improve.

By focusing their attention on these key areas—performance monitoring, curriculum mapping, curriculum change, instruction, professional development, data-based decision making, interventions for struggling students, and collaborative leadership and professional culture—educators at the dramatically improving school are able to continually progress toward higher levels of student learning. Although even doubling-performance schools and districts are at different stages along a continuum, the features of an improving school summarized above and in this book as a whole are the key elements that, when combined, significantly helped schools—elementary, middle, and high schools—move forward on a trajectory of continually improving student learning and literally doubling student performance over a medium-term time period.

3. THE KENNEWICK APPROACH TO DRAMATIC IMPROVEMENT

Rather than end the book with my own synthesis, I want to end with a synthesis of the overall strategy for producing large improvements that a leader in the Kennewick School District sent me.[2] His summary is a bit different from the above but reflects the same ideas. He wrote as follows:

We like to think there are three key elements to school improvement. They are assessment, curriculum, and instruction. The list of items below is one we have used to describe the key elements of our overall approach. It expands on the three key elements just mentioned.

1. *Leadership.* Leadership means that everyone in the district from the school board through the district office through the school buildings is focused on the same goal—in this case reading—and that focus does not change.

2. *A clear focus.* Schools are asked to fill many gaps in our society. Successful schools have clearly defined their focus. They do not react to every change in the tide. In the case of the Kennewick School District, we have determined that our primary focus is on developing reading skills. Because that focus is pervasive through every level of the organization, we are able to stay the course and resist pressure to move in another direction.

3. *Assessment.* In the book *Good to Great* the authors argue that before an organization can begin to improve it must confront the brutal reality of its current performance. Good, objective assessments, used systemwide have really helped our schools to define their reality.

   The second part of the assessment issue is to make the results public. Everyone needs to know how all elements of the organization are doing. In that way we can define the successful parts of that organization and work to determine what makes them successful.

   The final key to the assessment component is to have clear standards for the assessments that schools are held accountable to. The standards provide a direction and specific performance goals for schools.

   Our district assessment plan has been a crucial part of our success.

4. *Quality materials.* Curriculum materials do make a difference. The school district is responsible for helping schools find, use, and get trained in the very best curriculum materials available.

The teachers should not have to be the composer and conductor of the curriculum. Once teachers have the very best curriculum, their job is simply to conduct it elegantly so that it best meets the needs of the students.

5. *Time.* One of the expectations we set out is the amount of time spent on reading instruction. Our expectations are modeled after the best reading research. Once we established the concept of two hours of reading instruction in the primary grades, we made sure that teachers had the appropriate materials and the skills to use them well. Time is a key commodity in our schools, and we must use it strategically. Once we determine our focus, the use of time during the school day must reflect that focus.

6. *A systemic approach to instruction.* In our most successful schools, teachers do not work in isolation; they are a part of a team. The skills taught build from grade to grade and are tightly woven throughout the adopted program that is fully implemented. The curriculum is also fully used at each grade level allowing the teachers to work together in the planning of instruction and sharing students in specific instructional skill groups.

7. *Early effective intervention.* Before our reading initiative, interventions for struggling students were primarily a "second dose" of the same instructions students received in their classrooms. We have worked hard to use diagnostic assessments and find programs that will teach specifically to the skills deficit identified through the testing. One of the "dirty little secrets" was that we had to learn about effective interventions.

    Ideally, we can almost write prescriptions for our struggling students that identify specific weaknesses and the treatment to remediate the weaknesses.

8. *A sense of team.* It may almost be so obvious that we miss it, but schools that are effective see themselves as a team. They make decisions as a team, they support each other as a team, and they operate as a tight unit. It is more than the social events; the sense of team is pervasive in the instruction, organization, and everything that happens in the school. There is a strong sense of professional respect and support among and between all staff members.

9. *It's all about instruction.* The key factor in student achievement is instruction. All the elements above contribute to great instruction.

In addition we have set out some very specific expectations for instruction. For Kennewick teachers, that means that each lesson has a clear purpose, specific engagement strategies, appropriate rigor, and the results of the lesson can be measured.

We are very proud of the fact that in a recent survey our teachers indicated they knew and understood these expectations at very high levels.

NOTES

1. This synthesis is similar to but written differently from another recent study of system reform in large urban districts (Waters & Vargo, 2008).

2. Used with permission of Greg Fancher, assistant superintendent, elementary education, Kennewick School District, Kennewick, WA.

References

Alexander, K. L., & Entwisle, D. R. (1996). Schools and children at risk. In A. Booth & J. F. Dunn (Eds.), *Family-school links: How do they affect educational outcomes?* (pp. 67–89). Mahwah, NJ: Lawrence Erlbaum.

Aportela, A., & Goetz, M. (2008a). *Strategic management of human capital: New Leaders for New Schools.* Madison: University of Wisconsin, Wisconsin Center for Education Research, Consortium for Policy Research in Education, Strategic Management of Human Capital.

Aportela, A., & Goetz, M. (2008b). *Strategic management of human capital: Teach for America.* Madison: University of Wisconsin, Wisconsin Center for Education Research, Consortium for Policy Research in Education, Strategic Management of Human Capital.

Archibald, S. (2008). *Strategic management of human capital in Boston.* Madison: University of Wisconsin, Wisconsin Center for Education Research, Consortium for Policy Research in Education, Strategic Management of Human Capital.

Ascher, C. (1988). Summer school, extended school year, and year-round schooling for disadvantaged students. *ERIC Clearinghouse on Urban Education Digest, 42,* 1–2.

Austin, G. R., Roger, B. G., & Walbesser, H. H. (1972). The effectiveness of summer compensatory education: A review of the research. *Review of Educational Research, 42,* 171–181.

Betts, J. R., & Shkolnik, J. L. (1999). The behavioral effects of variations in class size: The case of math teachers. *Educational Evaluation and Policy Analysis, 21,* 193–215.

Black, P., & Wiliam, D. (1998). Inside the black box: Raising standards through classroom assessment. *Phi Delta Kappan, 80*(2), 139–144, 146–148.

Blankstein, A. (2004). *Failure is not an option: Six principles that guide student achievement in high performing schools.* Thousand Oaks, CA: Corwin.

Borman, G. D., & Boulay, M. (Eds.). (2004). *Summer learning: Research, policies, and programs.* Mahwah, NJ: Lawrence Erlbaum.

Borman, G. D., Rachuba, L., Hewes, G., Boulay, M., & Kaplan, J. (2001). Can a summer intervention program using trained volunteer teachers narrow the achievement gap? First-year results from a multi-year study. *ERS Spectrum, 19*(2), 19–30.

Boudett, K. P., City, E. A., & Murnane, R. (2007). *A step-by-step guide to using assessment results to improve teaching and learning.* Cambridge, MA: Harvard Education Press.

Boudett, K. P., & Steele, J. L. (2007). *Data wise in action: Stories of schools using data to improve teaching and learning.* Cambridge, MA: Harvard Education Press.

Boudreau, J., & Ramstad, J. (2007). *Beyond HR: The new science of human capital.* Boston: Harvard Business School.

Bransford, J., Brown, A., & Cocking, R. (1999). *How people learn.* Washington, DC: National Academy Press.

Chenoweth, K. (2007). *It's being done: Academic success in unexpected schools.* Cambridge, MA: Harvard Education Press.

Cohen, D. K., & Hill, H. C. (2001). *Learning policy: When state education reform works.* New Haven, CT: Yale University Press.

Cohen, P. A., Kulik, J. A., & Kulik, C. C. (1982). Educational outcomes of tutoring: A meta-analysis of findings. *American Educational Research Journal, 19*(2), 237–248.

Cohen, D. K., Raudenbush, S. W., & Ball, D. L. (2002). Resources, instruction, and research. In R. Boruch & F. Mosteller (Eds.), *Evidence matters: Randomized trials in education research* (pp. 80–119). Washington, DC: Brookings Institution.

Cooper, H., Charlton, K., Valentine, J. C., & L. Muhlenbruck, L. (2000). Making the most of summer school: A meta-analytic and narrative review. *Monographs of the Society for Research in Child Development, 65*(1, Serial No. 260), 1–118.

Cooper, H., Nye, B., Charlton, K., Lindsay, J., & Greathouse, S. (1996). The effects of summer vacation on achievement test scores: A narrative and meta-analytic review. *Review of Educational Research, 66,* 227–268.

Crawford, M. (2008). Think inside the clock. *Phi Delta Kappan, 90*(4), 251–255.

Cuban, L. (2008). The perennial reform: Fixing school time. *Phi Delta Kappan, 90*(4), 240–250.

Cunningham, P., & Allington, R. (1994). *Classrooms that work: They can all read and write.* New York: HarperCollins.

Darling-Hammond, L., & Richardson, N. (2009). Teaching learning: What matters? *Educational Leadership, 66*(5), 46–55.

Datnow, A., Park, V., & Kennedy, B. (2008). *Acting on data: How urban high schools use data to improve instruction.* Los Angeles: University of Southern California, Rossier School of Education, Center on Educational Governance.

Datnow, A., Park, V., & Wohlstetter, P. (2008). *Achieving with data: How high-performing schools systems use data to improve instruction for elementary students.* Los Angeles: University of Southern California, Rossier School of Education, Center on Educational Governance.

Donovan, S., & Bransford, J. (2005a). *How students learn: History in the classroom.* Washington, DC: National Research Council.

Donovan, S., & Bransford, J. (2005b). *How students learn: Mathematics in the classroom.* Washington, DC: National Research Council.

Donovan, S., & Bransford, J. (2005c). *How students learn: Science in the classroom.* Washington, DC: National Research Council.

Dubin, J. (2008). Reading Richmond: How scientifically based reading instruction is dramatically increasing achievement. *American Educator, 32*(3), 28–36.

DuFour, R., DuFour, R., Eaker, R., & Many, T. (2006). *Learning by doing: A handbook for professional learning communities at work.* Bloomington, IN: Solution Tree.

Elbaum, B., Vaughn, S., Hughes, M. T., & Moody, S. W. (1999). Grouping practices and reading outcomes for students with disabilities. *Exceptional Children, 65,* 399–415.

Elmore, R. F. (2002). *Bridging the gap between standards and achievement: The imperative for professional development in education.* Washington, DC: Albert Shanker Institute.

Elmore, R. F., & Burney, D. (1999). Investing in teacher learning: Staff development and instructional improvement. In L. Darling-Hammond & G. Sykes (Eds.), *Teaching as the learning profession: Handbook of policy and practice* (pp. 263–291). San Francisco: Jossey-Bass.

Evertson, C. M., & Randolph, C. H. (1989). Teaching practices and class size: A new look at the old issue. *Peabody Journal of Education, 67,* 85–105.

Farkas, G. (1998). Reading one-to-one: An intensive program serving a great many students while still achieving. In J. Crane (Ed.), *Social programs that work* (pp. 75–109). New York: Russell Sage.

Fashola, O. S. (1998). *Review of extended-day and after-school programs and their effectiveness* (Report No. 24). Washington, DC: Howard University. Center for Research on the Education of Students Placed at Risk (Crespar).

Fermanich, M., Mangan, M. T., Odden, A., Picus, L. O., Gross, B., & Rudo, Z. (2006). *Washington learns: Successful districts study.* Analysis prepared for the K–12 Advisory Committee of Washington Learns. (Available at http://www.lopassociates.com; go to State Studies).

Fielding, L., Kerr, N., & Rosier, P. (2004). *Delivering on the promise . . . of the 95% reading and math goals.* Kennewick, WA: New Foundation Press.

Finn, J. D., & Achilles, C. M. (1999). Tennessee's class size study: Findings, implications, misconceptions. *Educational Evaluation and Policy Analysis, 21*(2), 97–109.

Finn, J. D., Pannozzo, G. M., & Achilles, C. M. (2003). The "why's" of class size: Student behavior in small classes. *Review of Educational Research, 73*(3), 321–368.

Friedman, T. (2005). *The world is flat.* New York: Farrar, Straus & Giroux.

Fullan, M. (2001). *The new meaning of educational change.* New York: Teachers College Press.

Fullan, M. (2008). *What's worth fighting for in the principalship* (2nd ed.). New York: Teachers College Press.

Fullan, M., Hill, P., & Crévola, C. (2006). *Breakthrough.* Thousand Oaks, CA: Corwin.

Garet, M. S., Birman, B., Porter, A., Desimone, L., & Herman, R. (1999). *Designing effective professional development: Lessons from the Eisenhower program.* Washington, DC: U.S. Department of Education.

Goertz, M., & Levin, S. (2008). *Strategic management of human capital in New York City.* Madison: University of Wisconsin, Wisconsin Center for Education Research, Consortium for Policy Research in Education, Strategic Management of Human Capital.

Goetz, M., & Aportela, A. (2008). *Strategic management of human capital: The new teacher project.* Madison: University of Wisconsin, Wisconsin Center for Education Research, Consortium for Policy Research in Education, Strategic Management of Human Capital.

Goldenberg, C. (2008). Teaching English language learners. *American Educator, 32*(2), 8–23, 42–44.

Goldhaber, D., & Anthony, E. (2005). *Can teacher quality be effectively assessed? National board certification as a signal of effective teaching.* Washington, DC: Department of Education.

Goldhaber, D., Perry, D., & Anthony, E. (2004). The National Board for Professional Teaching Standards (NBPTS) process: Who applies and what factors are associated with NBPTS certification? *Educational Evaluation and Policy Analysis, 26*(4), 259–280.

Gordon, E. E. (2009). Five ways to improve tutoring programs. *Phi Delta Kappan, 90*(6), 440–445.

Gratton, L., Hope-Hailey, V., Stiles, P., & Truss, C. (1999). *Human resource strategy: Corporate rhetoric and human reality.* Oxford, UK: Oxford University Press.

Grubb, N. (2007). Dynamic inequality and intervention: Lessons from a small country. *Phi Delta Kappan, 89*(2), 105–114.

Gutierrez, R., & Slavin, R. (1992). Achievement effects of the nongraded elementary school: A best evidence synthesis. *Review of Educational Research, 62*(4), 333–376.

Halverson, R. (2003). Systems of practice: How leaders use artifacts to create professional community in schools. *Educational Policy and Analysis Archives, 11*(37). Accessible at http://epaa.asu.edu/epaa/v11n37

Heneman, H. G., III, & Kimball, S. (2008). *How to design new teacher salary structures.* Madison: University of Wisconsin, School of Education, Wisconsin Center for Education Research, Strategic Management of Human Capital (SMHC). Available at www.smhc-cpre.org/resources

Herman, R., Dawson, P., Dee, T., Greene, J., Maynard, R., Redding, S., et al. (2008). *Turning around chronically low-performing schools: A practice guide* (NCEE #2008-4020). Washington, DC: National Center for Education Evaluation and Regional Assistance, Institute of Education Sciences, U.S. Department of Education. Retrieved from http://ies.ed.gov/ncee/wwc/practiceguides

Heyns, B. (1978). *Summer learning and the effects of schooling.* New York: Academic Press.

Hiebert, J., Stigler, J. K., Jacobs, J. K., Givvin, K. B., Garnier, H., Smith, M., et al. (2005). Mathematics teaching in the United States today (and tomorrow): Results from the TIMSS 1999 video study. *Educational Evaluation & Policy Analysis, 27*(2), 111–132.

Hightower, A., Knapp, M., Marsh, J., & McLaughlin, M. (2002). *School districts and instructional renewal.* New York: Teachers College Press.

Hirsch, E. D., Jr. (1999a). *What your kindergartener needs to know: The core knowledge series.* Charlottesville, VA: Core Knowledge Foundation.

Hirsch, E. D., Jr. (1999b). *What your second grader needs to know: The core knowledge series.* Charlottesville, VA: Core Knowledge Foundation.

Hirsch, E. D., Jr. (1999c). *What your sixth grader needs to know: The core knowledge series.* Charlottesville, VA: Core Knowledge Foundation.

Hirsh, S., & Killion, J. (2007). *The learning educator: A new era of professional learning.* Oxford, OH: National Staff Development Council.

Hirsh, S., & Killion, J. (2009). When educators learn, students learn: Eight principles of professional learning. *Phi Delta Kappan, 90*(7), 464–469.

Hord, S., & Hirsh, S. (2009). The principal's role in supporting learning communities. *Educational Leadership, 66*(5), 22–23.

Informative Assessment. (2007/2008). *Educational Leadership, 65*(4).

Jordan, N. C. (2007). The need for number sense. *Educational Leadership, 65*(2), 63–66.

Joyce, B., & Calhoun, E. (1996). *Learning experiences in school renewal: An exploration of five successful programs.* Eugene, OR: ERIC Clearinghouse on Educational Management.

Joyce, B., & Showers, B. (2002). *Student achievement through staff development* (3rd ed.). Alexandria, VA: Association for Supervision and Curriculum Development.

Kellor, J. (2008, October 26). The time machine. *Chicago Tribune Magazine,* pp. 10–14, 20–21.

Kimball, S. (2008). *Strategic management of human capital in Chicago.* Madison: University of Wisconsin, Wisconsin Center for Education Research, Consortium for Policy Research in Education, Strategic Management of Human Capital.

Koppich, J. (2008). *Strategic management of human capital in Long Beach.* Madison: University of Wisconsin, Wisconsin Center for Education Research, Consortium for Policy Research in Education, Strategic Management of Human Capital.

Koppich, J., & Showalter, C. (2008). *A cross-case analysis of five districts.* Madison: University of Wisconsin, Wisconsin Center for Education Research, Consortium for Policy Research in Education, Strategic Management of Human Capital.

Kotter, J. P. (1996). *Leading change.* Boston: Harvard Business School Press.

Lawler, E., III. (2008). *Strategic talent management.* Madison: University of Wisconsin, Wisconsin Center for Education Research, Consortium for Policy Research in Education, Strategic Management of Human Capital.

Lawler, E. E., III, Boudreau, J. W., & Mohrman, S. A. (2006). *Achieving strategic excellence: An assessment of human resource organizations.* Stanford, CA: Stanford University Press.

Levin, J. D., & Quinn, M. (2003). *How we keep high-quality teachers out of urban classrooms.* New York: New Teacher Project. Retrieved from www.newteacherproject.org/report.html

Loucks-Horsley, S., Love, N., Stiles, K., Mundry, S., & Hewson, P. (2003). *Designing professional development for teachers of science and mathematics* (2nd ed.). Thousand Oaks, CA: Corwin.

Mangin, M., & Stoelinga, S. R. (2008). *Effective teacher leadership.* New York: Teachers College Press.

Mantzicopoulos, P., Morrison, D., Stone, E., & Setrakian, W. (1992). Use of the search/teach tutoring approach with middle-class students at risk for reading failure. *Elementary School Journal, 92,* 573–586.

Mason, D. A., & Burns, R. (1996). Simply no worse and simply no better may simply be wrong: A critique of Veenman's conclusion about multigrade classes. *Review of Educational Research, 66*(3), 307–322.

Mason, D. A., & Stimson, J. (1996). Combination and non-graded classes: Definitions and frequency in twelve states. *Elementary School Journal, 96*(4), 439–452.

Mathes, P. G., & Fuchs, L. S. (1994). The efficacy of peer tutoring in reading for students with mild disabilities: A best-evidence synthesis. *School Psychology Review, 23,* 59–80.

Milanowski, A. (2008). *Strategic management of human capital in Fairfax County.* Madison: University of Wisconsin, Wisconsin Center for Education Research, Consortium for Policy Research in Education, Strategic Management of Human Capital.

Miller, S. D. (2003). Partners in reading: Using classroom assistants to provide tutorial assistance to struggling first-grade readers. *Journal of Education for Students Placed at Risk, 8*(3), 333–349.

Murnane, R., & Levy, F. (1996). *Teaching the new basic skills.* New York: Free Press.

Musti-Rao, S., & Cartledge, G. (2007). Delivering what urban readers need. *Educational Leadership, 6*(2), 56–61.

Newmann, F., & associates. (1996). *Authentic achievement: Restructuring schools for intellectual quality.* San Francisco: Jossey-Bass.

Odden, A. (2008). *New teacher pay structures: The compensation side of the strategic management of human capital.* Madison: University of Wisconsin, Wisconsin Center for Education Research, Consortium for Policy Research in Education, Strategic Management of Human Capital.

Odden, A., & Archibald, S. (2001a). Committing to class-size reduction and finding the resources to implement it: A case study of resource reallocation in Kenosha, Wisconsin. *Education Policy Analysis Archives, 9*(30). Retrieved from http://epaa.asu.edu/epaa/v9n30.html

Odden, A., & Archibald, S. (2001b). *Reallocating resources: How to boost student achievement without spending more.* Thousand Oaks, CA: Corwin.

Odden, A. R., & Archibald, S. J. (2009). *Doubling student performance . . . and finding the resources to do it.* Thousand Oaks, CA: Corwin.

Odden, A., Archibald, S., Fermanich, M., & Gallagher, H. A. (2002). A cost framework for professional development. *Journal of Education Finance, 28*(1), 51–74.

Odden, A., & Kelly, J. A. (2008). *What is SMHC?* Madison: University of Wisconsin, Wisconsin Center for Education Research, Consortium for Policy Research in Education, Strategic Management of Human Capital.

Odden, A., & Picus, L. O. (2008). *School finance: A policy perspective* (4th ed.). New York: McGraw-Hill.

Odden, A., Picus, L. O., Archibald, S., Goetz, M., Aportela, A., & Mangan, M. T. (2007). *Moving from good to great in Wisconsin: Funding schools adequately and doubling student performance.* Madison: University of Wisconsin, Wisconsin Center for Education Research, Consortium for Policy Research in Education.

Organization for Economic Co-operation and Development. (2005). *Education At a Glance: OECD Indicators* 2005. Paris: Author.

Pavan, B. (1992). Recent research on nongraded schools: The benefits of non-graded schools. *Educational Leadership, 50*(2), 22–25.

Porter, A. C., Garet, M. S., Desimone, L. M., & Birman, B. F. (2003). Providing effective professional development: Lessons from the Eisenhower program. *Science Educator, 12*(1), 23.

Rice, J. K. (1999). The impact of class size on instructional strategies and the use of time in high school mathematics and science courses. *Educational Evaluation and Policy Analysis, 21,* 215–229.

Roberts, G. (2000). *Technical evaluation report on the impact of voyager summer programs.* Austin: University of Texas.

Schmidt, W. H. (1983). High school course-taking: A study of variation. *Journal of Curriculum Studies, 15*(2), 167–182.

Shanahan, T. (1998). On the effectiveness and limitations of tutoring in reading. *Review of Research in Education, 23,* 217–234.

Shanahan, T., & Barr, R. (1995). Reading recovery: An independent evaluation of the effects of an early instructional intervention for at-risk learners. *Reading Research Quarterly, 30*(4), 958–997.

Shulman, J. H., & Sato, M. (Eds.). (2006). *Mentoring teachers toward excellence: Supporting and developing highly qualified teachers.* San Francisco: Jossey-Bass with WestEd.

Silva, E. (2007). *On the clock: Rethinking the way schools use time.* Washington, DC: Education Sector.

Silva, E. (2008). The Benwood Plan: A lesson in comprehensive teacher reform. *Phi Delta Kappan, 89*(2), 127–134.

Slavin, R., Chamberlain, A., & Daniels, C. (2007). Preventing reading failure. *Educational Leadership, 65*(2), 22–27.

Smith, D., Wilson, B., & Corbett, R. (2009). Moving beyond talk. *Educational Leadership, 66*(5), 20–27.

Spillane, J. (2006). *Distributed leadership.* San Francisco: Jossey-Bass.

Spillane, J., Halverson, R., & Diamond, J. B. (2001). Investigating school leadership practice: A distributed perspective. *Educational Researcher, 30*(3), 23–27.

Stigler, J., & Hiebert, J. (1999). *The teaching gap: Best ideas from the world's teachers for improving education in the classroom.* New York: Free Press.

Supovitz, J. (2006). *The case for district-based reform.* Cambridge, MA: Harvard Education Press.

Supovitz, J., & Turner, H. M. (2000). The effects of professional development on science teaching practices and classroom culture. *Journal of Research in Science Teaching, 37*(9), 963–980.

Torgeson, J. K. (2004). Avoiding the devastating downward spiral. *American Educator, 28*(3), 6–19, 45–47.

Vandell, D. L., Pierce, K. M., & Dadisman, K. (2005). Out-of-school settings as a developmental context for children and youth. In R. Kail (Ed.), *Advances in child development and behavior* (Vol. 33, pp. 43–77). New York: Academic Press.

Veenman, S. (1995). Cognitive and noncognitive effects of multigrade and multiage classes: A best evidence synthesis. *Review of Educational Research, 65*(4), 319–381.

Wasik, B., & Slavin, R. E. (1993). Preventing early reading failure with one-to-one tutoring: A review of five programs. *Reading Research Quarterly, 28,* 178–200.

Waters, L. B., & Vargo, M. (2008). *Lessons learned in systemic district reform.* San Francisco: Springboard Schools.

Wei, R. C., Andree, A., & Darling-Hammond, L. (2009). How nations invest in teachers, *Educational Leadership, 66*(5), 28–33.

Wheldall, K., Coleman, S., Wenban-Smith, J., Morgan, A., & Quance, B. (1995). Teacher-child oral reading interactions: How do teachers typically tutor? *Educational Psychology, 12,* 177–194.

Wise, R. (2008). *Raising the grade: How high school reform can save our youth and nation.* San Francisco: Jossey-Bass.

Index

CORWIN

A SAGE Company

The Corwin logo—a raven striding across an open book—represents the union of courage and learning. Corwin is committed to improving education for all learners by publishing books and other professional development resources for those serving the field of PreK–12 education. By providing practical, hands-on materials, Corwin continues to carry out the promise of its motto: **"Helping Educators Do Their Work Better."**